STRANGE DETAILS

Writing **Architecture**

A project of the Anyone Corporation

STRANGE DETAILS

MICHAEL CADWELL

THE MIT PRESS

CAMBRIDGE, MASSACHUSETTS

LONDON, ENGLAND

© 2007 Massachusetts Institute of Technology

MIT Press books may be purchased at special quantity
discounts for business or sales promotional use.
For information, please email special_sales@mitpress.mit.edu
or write to Special Sales Department, The MIT Press, 55 Hay-
ward Street, Cambridge, MA 02142.

This book was set in Filosofia by Graphic Composition, Inc.
Printed and bound in the United States of America.

Library of Congress Cataloging-in-Publication Data

Cadwell, Mike, 1952–
    Strange details / Michael Cadwell.
        p. cm. —   (Writing architecture)
    Includes bibliographical references.
    ISBN-13: 978-0-262-53291-4 (pbk. : alk. paper)
    1. Architecture, Modern—20th century—Case studies.
    2. Building—Case studies. I. Title.
    NA680.C25 2007
                                                2006030939

10 9 8 7 6 5 4 3 2

"Making Strange" from *Selected Poems 1966–1987* by Seamus
Heaney. Copyright © 1990 by Seamus Heaney. Reprinted by
permission of Farrar, Straus and Giroux, LLC, for U.S.
permission and Faber and Faber for all other English-
language permissions.

CONTENTS

FOREWORD: A MURDER IN THE COURT

The title of Michael Cadwell's book, *Strange Details*, not only bor-
rows from poet Seamus Heaney, but also recalls the emphasis
placed by the Russian formalists on the question of "literari-
ness." Citing the ambiguous state of fact and fiction in both
historical and artistic documents, the formalists' aim was to
point out the "devices" that underlie all kinds of literary production. Focusing on form, they shifted their attention away
from content to the material reality of the text, and the transformation, deviation, or "violence" that was perpetrated on everyday
speech. Through deformation, they argued, ordinary language
was "made strange," resulting in defamiliarization (or estrange-
ment) that, in turn, would force an awareness of language—jolt-
ing the reader out the familiar state of distraction and into a
heightened self-consciousness.[1]

Drawing on this literary analogy, one might argue that a building is intensified through the elaboration of its own medium—*a
language of sticks and stones*—to induce a state of architecture. The
"material" that underlies architecture is somehow rooted in
construction and its details, and yet beguilingly, the devices that
engage the building practice are most often in tension with the
seemingly direct necessities of fabrication. Herein lies one of the
most fertile and debated topics in architectural theory: the subject of tectonics. At the heart of this debate is the dilemma posed
by the necessities of fabrication, which rarely coincide with the
intended expression of a building, even in those projects whose

1. Terry Eagleton, *Literary Theory* (Minneapolis: University of Minnesota Press, 1985).

authors profess an ethic of truthfulness or honesty to the facts of material construction.

Gottfried Semper addressed this dissonance when he identified the deceptive coincidence between aesthetics and physics in his description of rustication in traditional European architecture: "The stage by stage diminishing of the force implicit in the structural components, as you rise from the ground upward, seen everywhere in better architectural masonry, corresponds at the same time to a principle of beauty and dynamics."[2] Though his description may be seen as a mere integration of the two principles, Semper elsewhere differentiated them as "inner structure" and "artistic schema," articulating the difficulty of bringing technical facts into alignment with certain perceptual intuitions. As such, the "bearing of weight" is not simply a constructive problem of statics, but also a challenge for the construction of meaning. In his study of Semper, Michael Podro argues that "the architect can mark a real feature, suggest a fictive one, and in doing the latter may well involve masking some aspect of what is really there, as in the concealed breaks of the fluted columns or in a typical piece of medieval window masonry where the supporting colonettes are merely sculptural elaboration cut into the stone courses," further pointing to the rhetorical artifice in acts of construction.[3] Though Podro is here referring to an intended sleight of hand, he is also pointing to a more fundamental slippery relationship between construction facts and their corresponding aesthetic effects—even in cases where the expression of architecture and its method of fabrication are in closer alignment.

The relationship between the fictive and the factual certainly predates modern dilemmas, and the entasis of a Greek column

2. Quoted in Michael Podro, *The Critical Historians of Art* (New Haven, CT: Yale University Press, 1982), 48.

3. Podro, *The Critical Historians of Art*, 48.

has been similarly theorized. When, during the Renaissance, the architect's role was separated from that of the builders' guilds, there developed the relative autonomy of two disciplines in architecture: drawing and building. From the modern period to the contemporary scene, this takes on a new institutional guise in the way law defines the division of labor between architect and builder. The architect is charged with the design; the builder is responsible for the means and methods of its construction—as long as it remains faithful to "design intent." While this legal provision may seem a guarantor of design implementation in general, it significantly disempowers the architect and presents several theoretical predicaments. First, the law effectively severs the architect from the "specific" relationship she or he can construct between the technical specification of an artifact and its corollary effect—the assumption being that the architect's investment is in the image and its rhetoric, not in its constructive makeup. Second, it further problematizes the relationship between design intent and material construction by not offering a mechanism of control to determine the degree of association between them; this often happens through performance specifications, substitutions, and additional alternatives that are woven into contracts—as if to suggest that any detail or any material will suffice, so long as the general effect is delivered. Finally, the law also suggests a broader problem by cloaking the "many" means and methods available to the contractor, which are arguably the root substance of architectural production. How can one not, for instance, differentiate between a cast-in-place concrete wall and a precast one, without simultaneously broaching significant material and philosophical questions? Severing the architect from the means and methods of construction is somewhat like permitting the writer to use a certain vocabulary, but disassociating it from the very alphabet from which the text emerges.

In the 1970s and 1980s, when the emphasis on semantics, the production of meaning, and the communicative function of architecture took center stage, the question of construction waited in the wings. In many ways, both theory and the evolution of the legal system helped divorce architecture from the medium of construction. The most recent advancements in digital fabrication techniques have once again redistributed the power between the architect and builder—this, the result of the unmediated and immediate connection between drawing software and their corollary translation into fabrication paths. For these reasons, among others, Cadwell's book emerges at a critical moment, reasserting the centrality of the tectonic—with the detail as its accomplice—to take on a mission with significant cultural currency.

While Cadwell's immersion in his four subjects is broad—encompassing questions of the landscape, the cultural context, and the specifications of their architecture—his emphasis is on the strange place of the detail as manifested in the construction of four seminal buildings. The meticulous description of Mies's columns at the Farnsworth House is exemplary of the presence of the rhetorical question in Cadwell's conception of construction—precisely because of the multivalent ways in which the column can be read. If Semper's analysis of the effect of bearing weight identifies the girth of masonry as its proof, then Mies negates this very phenomenon to produce the illusion of weightlessness, denying the actual forces present on the columns at Farnsworth by having the columns cleverly slip outside the very roof they are meant to uphold. In addition, his refusal of bolts, and the effort put into grinding off the subsequent weld marks—in essence, to conceal the facts of construction—demonstrates the sophisticated tension and ambiguity in Mies's mischievous attitude toward construction. If the bolts would have held up a building just fine, then for Mies, only their elimination could uphold a principle of architecture. In this way, Mies's most paradigmatic invention at the Farnsworth House is a detail that he summarily proceeds to erase. The predicament, of course, is the result of the contradictory disciplinary mandates he has inherited: namely, to negotiate between technical and perceptual imperatives, which are at odds with each other. On the one hand, if he operates under the ethics of cost and efficiency, he must forgo the conceptual inversion that is offered by the effect of weightlessness. On the other hand, if he is to remain faithful to the rigors of the tectonic expression, then he must submit to a means and method that cleanses the steel of its surplus excretion—in essence, inducing an alignment between the purity of construction and its corollary effect, even if at a greater effort and cost. Mies's erasure of the welds is not simply rhetorical; they do not just *say* something, they *do* something. Imagine, if you will, a murder in the court of the Ryugen-in Temple, after which the perpetrator meticulously proceeds to rake the site of the crime. Is he covering his footsteps, or is he submitting to the rhetorical ethic of the Japanese garden? Mies, too, covers his footsteps, but he does so to uphold architecture, and his only crime is to expose the choices that construction has offered him.

In his writings, Cadwell unveils those choices, and he carefully balances the subtle and intricate ethics involved in the construction of architecture. He sets a task of identifying the difficult relationship between construction and the story of architecture—as if buildings could speak—using its details as witnesses to the narrative. But also, in recognizing the architects' medium, Cadwell foregrounds the importance of drawing as a form of communication: as a construction proscription, as expression, and as a mode of materializing the architect's peculiar and strange language. In turn, he extends the discourse on tectonics well beyond the "tired old insistence that construction must illustrate the structural strategies marshaled against gravity." Equally dissatisfied with

the obsessions of expression, semantics, and the symbolic function of architecture, Cadwell calls for a broader reading of the
discipline linking aspects of construction, landscape, drawing,
and perception in a more complex narrative that repositions a
vision of architecture in the world, even if at the cost of killing an
older one.

Nader Tehrani

ACKNOWLEDGMENTS

I am indebted to three institutions that assisted me during different stages of my writing *Strange Details*. The Graham Foundation
provided financial support for illustrations. The Austin E. Knowlton School of Architecture and the College of Engineering at The
Ohio State University provided additional financial support and a
sabbatical. And the American Academy in Rome provided an extraordinary environment for my sabbatical, one that supported the
growth of a few ruminations into the book that you have before you.

It is people who make the difference, however. For a number
of years, Robert Livesey has cultivated the Austin E. Knowlton
School of Architecture as a kind of architectural seedbed. I am indebted to his unflagging efforts and to the numerous colleagues
that he has gathered over the years: Jane Amidon, Jeffrey Kipnis,
Jose Oubrerie, and Stephen Turk, to name just a few. Diana Livesey
also read early drafts of these essays and clarified their prose. At
the American Academy in Rome, I landed amid another community, one that embraced the unique combination of low comedy
and high endeavor upon which I seem to depend. Led with be-
nign forbearance by Lester Little and Lella Gandini (and, less
officially, by the exuberant machinations of Pat Olezko), this crew
is too numerous to enumerate, but I must thank Clytie Alexander,
Peter and Julie Boswell, Darcy Grigsby, Louis Guida, Amy Hauft,
Tom Leader, Paul Lewis, Catherine McCurrach, Todd Olson, Jack
Risley, Jonathan Thornton, Craig Verzone, and Cristina Woods.

I also thank Eeva-Liisa Pelkonen for her suggestions during
the early drafts of this book, Cynthia Davidson for her support

during the book's later stages of development, and Kathleen Caruso at The MIT Press for her editorial expertise during the book's production. Finally, I thank Luke Kautz for tracking down illustrations, and Jane Murphy, who visited buildings with me and suffered my postulations and prevarications with equanimity, and to whom I dedicate this book.

INTRODUCTION, "MAKING STRANGE"

I stood between them,
the one with his traveled intelligence
and tawny containment,
his speech like the twang of a bowstring,

and another, unshorn and bewildered
in the tubs of his wellingtons,
smiling at me for help,
faced with this stranger I'd brought him.

Then a cunning middle voice
came out of the field across the road
saying, 'Be adept and be dialect,
tell of this wind coming past the zinc hut,

call me sweetbriar after the rain
or snowberries cooled in the fog.
But love the cut of this traveled one
and call me also the cornfield of Boaz.

Go beyond what's reliable
in all that keeps pleading and pleading,
these eyes and puddles and stones,
and recollect how bold you were

when I visited you first
with departures you cannot go back on.'
A chaffinch flicked from an ash and next thing
I found myself driving the stranger

through my own country, adept
at dialect, reciting my pride
in all that I knew, that began to make strange
at that same recitation.
—Seamus Heaney, "Making Strange"

In the spring and summer of 1999, I had the good fortune to be a fellow at the American Academy in Rome. My proposal was to study the work of the Italian architect Carlo Scarpa, whose small gallery at the Querini Stampalia Foundation had baffled me when I had stumbled upon it in Venice two years earlier. Scarpa's intricate construction techniques, I came to believe, had loosened my moorings, and I was confident that I could reground myself in the gallery if I dissected its construction. During that spring, I drew Scarpa's construction details, not only at the Querini Stampalia, but elsewhere in Venice and Italy: Passagno, Verona, Treviso, and Palermo. It seemed a simple matter to tape my collection of crisp ink drawings to the white sunlit walls of my spacious Academy studio and allow their logic to reveal itself.

The drawings refused to cooperate. No matter how I arranged the details on the walls, they resisted an order. I returned to books that informed my original assumptions—Edward R. Ford's *The Details of Modern Architecture*, Kenneth Frampton's *Studies in Tectonic Culture*, and Francesco Dal Co and Giuseppe Mazzariol's *Carlo Scarpa, The Complete Works*—but I could not make the connections that I had anticipated between a conventional phenomenology and Scarpa's heralded mastery of materials. Instead, my drawings confronted me with a catalog of liquefying motifs: steel joined at odd intervals, concrete spilled out of concatenated forms, and stone cut in labyrinthine patterns. In spite of its seductive materiality and its persistent intricacy, I could not appreciate this catalog as anything other than one of sensual compulsion, as if architecture, too, might offer guilty pleasures that degenerated into tired mechanics. Reasoning that a broader critical view was necessary, I equipped myself with Neil Leach's collection of seminal twentieth-century essays, *Rethinking Architecture*. Again, to no avail. Illuminating as the essays were, my efforts to turn them toward Scarpa's details offered only glimmerings of depths that I could not fathom and, more often, didactic schemes that flattened the constructions into a dim, arid lifelessness. The drawings were stubborn; they cast me off.

My respite from this ordeal was a collection of Seamus Heaney's poetry. In particular, I found myself rereading Heaney's poem "Making Strange," first as a distraction and then with growing intent.

Heaney writes "Making Strange" in the first person and recalls a visit to a familiar village, perhaps the village of his youth. As the poem opens, we find Heaney standing between an intellectual colleague "with his traveled intelligence and tawny containment" and an old acquaintance, "unshorn and bewildered in the tubs of his wellingtons." Although the former is more articulate—"his speech like the twang of a bowstring" in contrast to the latter's mute "smiling at me for help"—it is a third voice that calls to Heaney. This "cunning middle voice" has an indeterminate origin, from "out of the field across the road." We know that it comes from neither the acquaintance's village nor the colleague's milieu, and we sense that it might negotiate between the two. The ensuing lines support our intimation. The voice conjures a pastoral of zinc hut, sweetbriar, and snowberries and links this scene with the Old

Testament story of Boaz and Ruth. With this linkage, the voice conjoins Ireland with a biblical terrain where a salubrious landscape also masked generations of conflict. Heaney not only stands between personifications of native intelligence and cultural sophistication, but also must provide them with a unifying poetic vision.

We know this third voice is not Heaney's. He describes it in measured terms; this "cunning middle voice" may be too clever or compromised, and its tone veers between that of a muse and a pedant. The voice's opening advisement to "be adept and be dialect" reinforces its proscriptive tone, and its abrupt reference to Boaz (adept), amended to the more vivid pastoral (dialect), does not give rise to a new imaginative landscape. More strident with each line, the voice admonishes Heaney to abandon his dependence on agrarian imagery—"Go beyond what's reliable / in all that keeps pleading and pleading"—and then mocks him with a common pastoral that exhausts vision itself, "these eyes and puddles and stones." The voice leaves Heaney with a reprimand: "'and recollect how bold you were / when I visited you first / with departures you cannot go back on.'"

Nature snaps Heaney out of his reverie midstanza, "a chaffinch flicked from an ash," and he discovers that he is "driving the stranger through [his] own country." Heaney is now "adept at dialect" in distinction from the middle voice's "adept and . . . dialect." That is, Heaney has come into possession of a voice that fuses, rather than conjoins, an intimate vernacular with cultural sophistication. Heaney describes this voice, but it is important to note that he does not give it voice; we do not know what he tells the stranger. The poem outlines an imaginative project while its results are still at large. Heaney can only suggest the project's central task with the poem's title and its closing lines, "to make strange / at that same recitation." We can surmise, however, that Heaney's new voice will not make a world intelligible by returning it to the familiar or by linking it to an existing order. Heaney's voice will render a new imaginative territory compelling by conserving its strangeness.

In successive readings, I realized that Heaney's poem evoked what was at play in Scarpa's work, and by evoking it rather than labeling it kept that play alive. Scarpa, too, made strange. As my drawings insisted, Scarpa made strange with the most resistant aspect of architecture—construction. Scarpa does not anchor us with construction conventions no matter how elaborately construed. Nor, for that matter, does he reaffirm terra firma as we habitually assume it (or question it with the tropes of modernism). Instead, construction liquefies at the Querini Stampalia, and we are cast adrift, into a kind of liquid ambience. What I had dismissed as a collection of fetishes, I came to understand as a coherently constructed world that was, nevertheless, persistently strange. I was right to feel unmoored; I was wrong to resist it.

Since my fellowship, I have led a graduate seminar on construction at the Austin E. Knowlton School of Architecture at The Ohio State University. My students and I have detected a similar strangeness in the construction of several other buildings, and three in particular: the light wood frame of Frank Lloyd Wright's Jacobs House, the welded steel frame of Mies van der Rohe's Farnsworth House, and the reinforced concrete of Louis I. Kahn's Yale Center for British Art. The idiosyncrasies of this strangeness are the subject of the following essays; yet three recurring themes can be outlined here, themes that are also integral to Heaney's poem.

First, these are accomplished architects whose work transforms. Much as "Making Strange" is a transitional poem for Heaney, these buildings mark pivotal moments in the careers of their architects, when the architects also challenge their hardwon facility. Given the experience of the architects, we cannot dismiss these strange construction details as youthful indulgences any more than we can reduce them to pragmatic solutions. And, notwithstanding the social prerequisites of building and the risk of reducing art to biography, we must acknowledge the personal and professional histories of the architects who developed these details.

Second, like the mature voice that Seamus Heaney projects for himself, these architects each fuse culture with vernacular, a vernacular that I translate in architectural terms as inherited construction norms. Scarpa, Wright, Mies, and Kahn are not "adept *and* dialect"—possessed by a set of ideas for which construction is a more or less cumbersome mode of illustration. Rather, they are "adept *at* dialect"—attuned to cultural currents that reconfigure the rudimentary facts of construction and create a subtle yet undeniable shift in a building's dumb physicality. In this regard, the architects step ahead of the poet for each has built what the poet can only project. My intention for these essays is neither ideological nor, in the strictest sense of the term, critical, but one of appreciation: to revisit the strangeness of these buildings, to exhume their tactics of construction, and to evoke their all-embracing affects.

Finally, Heaney's reverie on inheritance and culture informs his emerging poetic voice, but the intercession of nature brings his voice to life. Nature does not prod gently. Nature startles Heaney, and he cannot capture it with a dewy pastoral such as that of the poem's middle verses. The simplicity of the phrase "a chaffinch flicked from an ash" is deceptive. Its consonants have a percussive force, while its syntax is ambiguous, lacking a defining "tree" and giving rise to images of a phoenix and an expiring cigarette as well as a flushed bird. Heaney now confronts a natural world that is fleeting, ambivalent; it is charred and hints at vague threats. Heaney seems dazed, as if dully reporting someone else's actions: "next thing / I found myself driving the stranger / through my own country." He dismisses himself as if he were a schoolboy "reciting [his] pride / in all that [he] knew," and the closing lines "that began to make strange / at that same recitation" have no clear referent, extending beyond Heaney to include the chaffinch, the country, and the poetic act itself. Nature is strange, and its strangeness infects.

Something very similar happens in the work of Scarpa, Wright, Mies, and Kahn. Nature asserts itself upon each architect in different guises, yet always as something foreign, a kind of volatile atmosphere, rather than as something familiar, affording a comfortable ground. For the architects as well as the poet, nature unmoors exhausted cultural ideas, constricted analytical procedures, and outmoded production techniques. All these, Heaney intimates in his poem and I realized in Rome, are swept asunder like so much flotsam and jetsam. For Scarpa, Wright, Mies, and Kahn, an awakening to nature's strangeness forces a new sense of the world, one that we can detect in their configurations of the world's materials—their strange details.

STRANGE DETAILS

1.1

Querini Stampalia Foundation
from Campiello Santa Maria
Formosa

1 SWIMMING AT THE QUERINI STAMPALIA FOUNDATION

Late in his career, Le Corbusier invested his considerable ener-
gies in an ill-fated, yet influential, design for a civic hospital in
Venice. During one of his visits to the archipelago in 1964, Le
Corbusier broke from his responsibilities and spent a relaxed
afternoon as a tourist, sightseeing. In the course of his peram-
bulations, Le Corbusier found his way to the recently renovated
Querini Stampalia Foundation where, gazing about in admiration,
he exclaimed, "Qui est ce beau artisan?" "Carlo Scarpa," his hosts
informed him.

Le Corbusier asks his question, we can assume, with mixed
intent. Scarpa sparks the master's curiosity, but Le Corbusier
assumes that Scarpa is something less than an architect: more of
a tradesman, or perhaps an interior decorator. Le Corbusier's
assumption is a common one, however. What is striking in much
of Scarpa's work is the attention that he lavished on the smallest
detail: the deep hues of a plaster panel's finish, the polished brass
accent to a steel pivot joint, the glazed tile inset in a rough, sitecast
concrete wall. Such eloquent phrasings draw us forward even as we

wonder, Does this collection cohere into something greater than its exquisite parts or does it remain a trove of jewelry, lapidary and testifying to exquisite taste, but finally more craft than art?

Little known in Europe during his lifetime, Scarpa was virtually unknown in America. Scarpa's oeuvre is small, stultified by a sluggish Italian postwar economy and a politicized architectural community. It was not until the 1970s that an emerging generation of American architects gravitated to Scarpa. Steven Holl, Billy Tsien, George Ranalli, Michael Rotundi, Eric Owen Moss— for these and a host of other young practitioners, Scarpa's allure was multivalent. His attentive detailing countered the banal expediencies of late modernism and the superficial excesses of postmodernism. His deft interventions into historic buildings rebuked late modernism's self-righteous bulldozings and postmodernism's trite panderings. His insistence upon the phenomenological countered the linguistic bias of prevailing architectural theory. Finally, his marginal professional status seemed to provide an authentic alternative to the corporate entanglements of the architectural status quo. Scarpa, in America at least, had arrived.

My introduction to the work of Carlo Scarpa was more ambivalent. Attending architecture school during the ascendancy of Scarpa's reputation, I did not discover his work on my own, but had it pressed upon me by my teachers (never a good start, however well-intended). I was a beginner and I searched, with varying degrees of desperation, for what I imagined to be a more fundamental approach to architecture. Scarpa's work, whatever else might be said about it, is not easy, and its broader implications are indecipherable if one has access to only a scattering of photographs and plans. I felt as if I were learning the English language and my teachers had dropped *Finnegans Wake* in my lap. "What is this?" I asked before tossing it.

It was not until much later, when lost in the labyrinth of Venice, that I stumbled upon the Querini Stampalia Foundation and came under Scarpa's spell. Drifting in the foundation's little gallery, I was transported: how and to where I did not know, but I knew that I was . . . elsewhere. It was later still that I came to understand how Scarpa cast this spell: how he liquefied materials and how, in doing so, he sometimes gave rise to an all-embracing spatial affect that unmoors us from the earth, leaving us to swim in a liquid ambience. Scarpa's sensibility, especially for an architect, was fundamentally strange. It was aquatic.

I will return to Venice and the Querini Stampalia Foundation in the course of this chapter, for it is there that Scarpa's aquatic sensibility reaches high tide. Now, however, I make a brief detour to a key passage in the writing of the philosopher Martin Heidegger. Scarpa was a profoundly sensual architect, a purveyor of phenomena, and Heidegger, perhaps more than any twentieth-century philosopher, attempted a phenomenological reading of the world. My detour will not attempt an exhaustive exegesis of Heidegger's work, but will serve only as a rhetorical device that reveals the exceptional world that is Venice. Venice, it seems to me, offers a key to understanding the fundamental break between the sensibility of Scarpa and those of his contemporaries.

A central concept in Heidegger's work is that of dwelling. Dwelling, in Heidegger's lexicon, is not simply inhabiting the earth, mindlessly going about the business of life. Dwelling transcends habit and lands lightly within the poetics of being, a profound appreciation of and involvement with the elemental qualities of the concrete. Architecture, for Heidegger, becomes a powerful metaphor for how we set truth to work and thereby reveal the essential qualities of the world. "For building," Heidegger writes, "is not merely a means and a way toward dwelling—to build is in itself already to dwell."

In his essay "The Origin of the Work of Art," Heidegger provides his now well-known example of dwelling, a Greek temple:

> Standing there, the building rests on the rocky ground. This resting of the work draws up out of the rock the mystery of that rock's clumsy yet spontaneous support. Standing there, the building holds its ground against the storm raging above it and so first makes the storm manifest in its violence. The luster and gleam of the stone, though itself apparently glowing only by the grace of the sun, yet first brings to light the light of the day, the breadth of the sky, the darkness of the night. The temple's firm towering makes visible the invisible space of air. The steadfastness of the work contrasts with the surge of the surf, and its own repose brings out the raging of the sea. Tree and grass, eagle and bull, snake and cricket first enter into their distinctive shapes and thus come to appear as what they are. The Greeks early called this emerging and rising in itself and in all things phusis. It clears and illuminates, also, that on which and in which man bases his dwelling. We call this ground the earth.

This is a beautiful passage. It is compromised, surely, by Heidegger's political involvements, his fabrication of origins for the slippery ebb and flow of language, and his drive to invest things with ontological significance; he will not let things be, he stuffs them with being (and being with a capital *B*). Nevertheless, I point out a very simple thing: Heidegger is depicting the earth as a stable condition, a ground from which work inevitably extends. Work, it also seems inevitable, that will rise to the sky.

Thus, the temple "draws up out of the rock the mystery of that rock's clumsy yet spontaneous support." There is, furthermore, an inviolate pair of opposites to be negotiated, the sky acting as an intemperate partner to the earth's stalwart presence. And even though Heidegger continues his description with the admonition that the earth "is not to be associated with the idea of a mass of matter deposited somewhere, or with the merely astronomical idea of a planet," the momentum of his rhetoric of earth and sky and his imagery of paired oppositions—"tree and grass, eagle and bull, snake and cricket"—carries him forward. He closes this paragraph with the injunction, "Earth is that whence the arising brings back and shelters everything that arises without violation. In the things that arise, earth is present as the sheltering agent." It is hard to imagine otherwise. The way we inhabit the earth in even our most distracted moments—our feet on the ground, our heads lifted skyward—seems to substantiate this assumption.

Indeed, Kenneth Frampton, in his seminal and encyclopedic study of modern architecture, *Studies in Tectonic Culture*, bases a large part of his argument for a phenomenology of architecture on "the unavoidably earthbound nature of building." It seems self-evident. Even the two canonical works of twentieth-century architecture that spring free of the ground—Frank Lloyd Wright's FallingWater and Le Corbusier's Villa Savoye—depend in large part upon the fact that they spring from something to something. FallingWater leaps from the rock of a Pennsylvania hillside, and Villa Savoye lifts itself above the plain of Poissy; both leave the earth for the sky, but in that very movement reaffirm the earth and the sky as opposites, as poles in a dialectic. It is hard to imagine otherwise.

Of course, there is Venice. We first glimpse Venice across the lagoon, from a boat. The buildings seem suspended in a field of sea and sky, each reflecting the other and finally dissolving into hues of blue and gray. Where is the earth now? A thin, barely perceptible line upon which the buildings cannot possibly depend. The buildings float, fantastically; they cannot be grounded because there is no ground. But as we step to the campo, the pavers seem firm enough, the buildings seem stable enough, and we repress our eerie intuition, accustomed as we are to the reassurances of terra firma. Yet this, history reveals, is denial.

Venice was settled early in the fifth century. With the fall of Rome, hordes of vandals swept over the northern Italian frontier and dispersed the populations from Aquilegia to Padua; this diaspora eventually rerooted itself among the traders and fishermen of the Realtine Islands. Islands is a euphemism in this case; the Realtine Islands were nothing more than mudflats. Gradually, the citizenry developed techniques for stabilizing this primordial muck by piling it and damming it behind stone retaining walls, stealing from the lagoon until Venice grew to four times the size of the original flats. The campos themselves served as ingenious systems for potable water: rainwater penetrated the unmortared pavers, flowed to box drains that punctuated the campo, filtered through the sand below, and collected in wells set atop the impermeable clay that lined the entire system. Campos are not simply public squares in Venice; they are cisterns as well, floating cisterns.

Builders also developed ingenious strategies for supporting the fiction of the earth in palazzo construction. They pounded hundreds of wooden pilings through layers of unstable soil and anchored them firmly into the *caranto*, a lower layer of more solid clay and sand. Atop these piling mats, builders fashioned palazzos of stuccoed brick with wooden floor and ceiling beams and tiled roofs, veiling the more affluent of these concoctions with delicate filigrees of marble. The farther Venice grew into the lagoon, of course, the less accessible the *caranto* was to the reach of pilings. By the sixteenth century, builders discarded pilings altogether and replaced them with a more expeditious system of interwoven brick, mortar, stone, and wooden planks, a kind of composite barge upon which the buildings floated. In Venice, buildings do not spring from the earth—they tether themselves to the mud below, or they hover above it. In Venice, buildings do not spring from the earth because in Venice the earth does not exist.

The precariousness of this position is apparent everywhere. The dampness of the canals creeps up the walls, causing the stucco veneers to flake off like dead skin to reveal the brick structure beneath, bricks that are crumbling from the same incessant moisture. Buildings are reflected in the water, an interminable doubling until, on a calm day, it is difficult to tell which is the more real: the flickering reflection or the crumbling original. There is a crude humor to this relationship of building to site; the doubling inspires a Venetian slapstick whereby canal water rebukes ponderous buildings, sending them back their reflection like a pie in the face. If we continue to repress these worrisome observations, the flooding tides of the *acqua alta* sweep in like an unwanted dream, reasserting the dominance of the water and threatening to sweep the whole confection into the lagoon, erasing that beautiful, thin, feeble line forever.

The press often portrays the *acqua alta* as if it were a Disneyesque spectacle induced for the amusement of tourists. However, the effects of the *acqua alta* on Venice have been disastrous and were particularly horrendous in the successive floods of the late 1950s and early 1960s, culminating in the devastation of November 1966. Scarpa himself described "the drifting debris of bits of timber, seaweed, algae, clots of tar, organic impurities, fetid froth, and 'vile pottery' swirling in eddies in a backwater of Venice with, at its center, half a calf's head, cruelly carved by the butcher's knife; along the lines of that map of bile anatomy which delimits the better cuts of meat from the offal." This is a cityscape that is also a landscape, both listing toward entropy or, to use the Latin term that Scarpa as a devout Catholic might have used, *in extremis:* at the point of death, at the moment of revelation.

Carlo Scarpa was born in Venice on June 2, 1906. His family moved to Vicenza two years later, but returned when Scarpa was thirteen and entered the Academia di Belle Arti. Scarpa left Venice for the hillsides of Asolo in 1962, escaping the floods as work progressed at the Querini Stampalia Foundation. By this time, he was in his mid-fifties, a mature architect with substantial gifts. First among these gifts was Scarpa's mastery of materials, a facility evident in his designs for the Cappellin, and later Venini, glassworks on the Venetian island of Murano. Murano has been a center for glassmaking since the tenth century, and glass has become so common that we forget its paradoxical genesis. Glass, in spite of its transparent capacities, is primarily made of sand, and, in spite of its solid appearance, glass has no fixed melting point and an open, noncrystalline microstructure; it is a supercooled liquid. For two decades (1927–1947), Scarpa collaborated with Murano's fabled glassworkers, developing new techniques: *sommerso* layered the glass with pellucid depths, *corroso* added a glimmering texture, *battuto* ground the glass to a battered surface, and *tessuti velati* wove the glass into varied bands. Scarpa seemed to return this peculiarly Venetian combination of sand and liquid to its fluid state; patterned polychromes reflect and waver deep within voluptuous forms caught midsurrender. Scarpa knew glass first, and its lessons stayed with him.

Scarpa also had a remarkable empathy for historical artifacts, which led to extensive museum renovations at the Palazzo Abetellis in Palermo, the Accademia in Venice, the Canova Plaster-Cast Gallery in Possagna, and the Castelvecchio in Verona, as well as numerous installations of contemporary art, most notably at successive Venice Biennales. Scarpa's affinity was extraordinary and cannot be attributed only to having matured in a city that is itself an extensive museum. Scarpa often displaced the artwork—paintings onto elaborate easels hinged with brass, books into delicate-legged vitrines, sculpture boarded onto bargelike bases or drifting from extended steel armatures—so that they leave the hygienic remove of the museum world without completely entering our own. We puzzle over possible connections, and not only as an intellectual exercise. Conclusive anchorings to the ground exhaust themselves with elaborate hesitations or cloak themselves behind shadowed reveals. It is as if the artifacts also have stepped to the campo, but with great distrust. We can only surmise that Scarpa shared this distrust; that, as an architect, he questioned what most of us assume: How do I attach to the ground if it is not there?

We must also acknowledge Scarpa's admiration of the work of Frank Lloyd Wright, an influence overcome, after many false starts, in Scarpa's exquisite Olivetti Showroom on the Piazza San Marco. Yet again a proviso asserts itself. The Istrian limestone treads that cascade from the showroom's second to first floor recall Wright's concrete cantilevers at FallingWater, but Wright abstracts the landscape's cascade in crisp geometries while Scarpa shapes the stone into the bends and folds of successive waves. Wright and Scarpa pass each other, certainly, but they are going in different directions: Wright from liquid to solid, Scarpa from solid to liquid.

It is a testimony to the unorthodox nature of his career that in 1956 Scarpa won the Olivetti commission in conjunction with the National Prize for Design and, in that same year, the Venetian Order of Architects sued him for illegally practicing as an architect. Although Scarpa taught at the Venice School of Architecture throughout his life, he never received an architectural degree himself. Of course, any biography of Scarpa is doomed to be cursory. Scarpa amassed a library of over four thousand volumes, and he described himself as "a man of Byzantium who came to Venice by way of Greece." Such an amniotic trip might include all the major monuments of Western (and, by implication, Eastern) civilization . . . and could only be made by water. Scarpa was born on water, matured on water, and built on water. Not land. Unlike his terrestrial contemporaries, Scarpa's was an aquatic sensibility, saturated by Venice.

———

The history of the Querini Stampalia Foundation is peculiarly Venetian. Built between 1513 and 1523, the palace of the Querini Stampalia family was of the standard Venetian type: a four-story affair with storage directly accessing the canal, a *piano nobile* above for business transactions, and top floors providing private quarters for the family. To the rear of the palazzo was a garden surrounded by high protective walls. The fortunes of the family obviously prospered for the family supplied a doge in 1694, Silvestro Falier, who was married to Elisabetta Querini. In 1869, Count Giovanni Querini Stampalia died and willed the palace and its collection to "promote study of useful disciplines and national and foreign knowledge." When the Foundation's director, Giuseppe Mazzariol, enlisted Scarpa in 1958, the task was to renovate the ground floor, which successive encroachments of the *acqua alta* had badly damaged. The area would become a gallery space, but would also need to accommodate future floods.

We need not elaborate upon the successive stages of the renovation other than to note that Scarpa's painstaking method of working required the forbearance and engagement of a patron. Mazzariol seems to have been ideal in both regards, his patience matched only by what must have been a profound critical appreciation for Scarpa's work. Scarpa's sole draftsperson, Lucino Zinatto, described the balance well: how "Scarpa would get an idea in an afternoon and spend the next three months refining it" and, at the same time, how the project "became a game—they obviously found it a pleasure to work together." Indeed, Mazzariol oversaw the completion of the garden because Scarpa was, by then, involved in other projects. If the relationship of architect to client seems of another age, the relationship Scarpa enjoyed with the construction team certainly was. As Richard Murphy elaborates in his meticulous study of the project:

> *The absence of industrialization has prolonged crafts-manship [in Venice]. It is a characteristic of the city that was an absolute prerequisite for Scarpa, essential for the success of any of his projects. Not only did he demand and expect a high quality of craftsmanship, he also tried to use the same team again and again, both in Venice and be-yond. Scarpa needed to communicate verbally and picto-rially with the craftsman. He would have loathed the modern legalistic division between design activity and construction: for him the two could not be autonomous. The "team" for Querini Stampalia was the same as for many other projects: Servevio Anfodillo for joinery work, Paolo Zanon for steelwork, Silvio Fassi poured concrete and Eugenio de Luigi produced his famous Venetian "stucco lucido" for the internal plaster panels.*

The scheme seems straightforward: a small bridge spans the Campiello Santa Maria Formosa, over the Rio Santa Maria Canal, to the ground floor of the palazzo. Scarpa arranged the ground-floor rooms enfilade to open to the rear garden. As is true of most of Scarpa's commissions, the scale of the intervention is modest: the enclosed area measures only 40 x 65 feet while the garden measures only 40 x 80 feet. In spite of the small scale of the intervention, Scarpa took great pains to differentiate three circulation paths. An honorific way leads directly from the canal, up a set of stairs to the main gallery, and on to the garden. A more common public way crosses the bridge to a foyer and then joins the honorific way to gallery and garden. Finally, a separate service route links

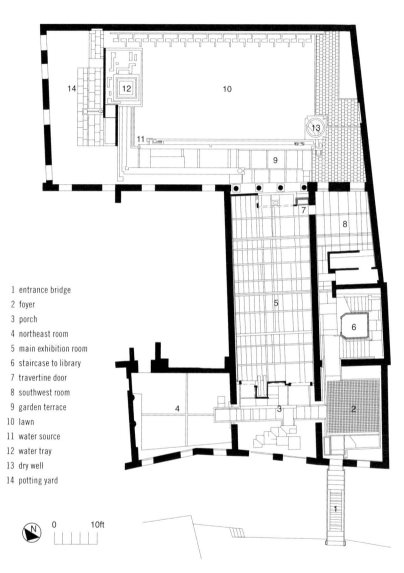

1 entrance bridge
2 foyer
3 porch
4 northeast room
5 main exhibition room
6 staircase to library
7 travertine door
8 southwest room
9 garden terrace
10 lawn
11 water source
12 water tray
13 dry well
14 potting yard

N   0   10ft

1.2

Plan

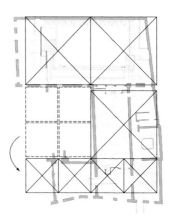
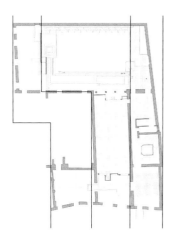

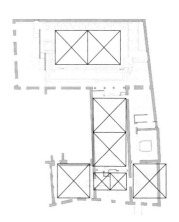
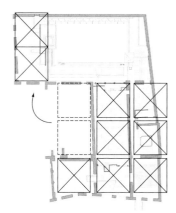

1.3

Plan diagrams: four-square, program,
nine-square, and double-squares

the alley through a gate to the garden and through a door to the service closet.

The Querini Stampalia dispels a common misperception that Scarpa lacked the discipline to maintain clear organizational structure in his projects. Scarpa divided the renovation into an honorific central zone flanked by a public zone to the right and a service zone to the left. Scarpa's organization also describes the standard formal plan geometries of a four-square (wherein the missing fourth square is quartered and shifted to the front entry system) and a nine-square (wherein the missing eighth and ninth service squares are shifted to the potting area of the garden). There is one diagram remaining, however; double squares flicker through the entry porch, gallery, and garden. Instead of the simple affirmation of one square with its reassuring insistence upon a center, two squares exist, one seemingly the shadow of the other, its double, or its reflection. In any case, a strange dislocation lurks within the organization as if Scarpa inscribed solid geometries onto an unstable liquid surface.

And here, it seems to me, is the more accurate observation to be made regarding Scarpa's working method: that the plan was a loose affiliation of geometries that was both immediately recognizable and, upon closer observation, vaguely unsettling, while the details maintained their unique figurative resonance, a resonance independent of technical expediency or larger schematic absolutes. Running counter to the prevailing modernist notions of his day, Scarpa did not insist upon the plan as the generator of the project, formulating a logic that commanded all aspects of a building. Rather, Scarpa deployed the plan as a kind of straight man, mute except for a few sly asides, who allowed the details to come to center stage with all their dramatic flourishes and comic upsets. For Scarpa, ornament—the scourge of doctrinaire modernism—is the key. Very well, let's take a walk.

The Querini Stampalia borders the small Campiello Santa Maria Formosa, not far from Piazza San Marco, but sufficiently remote from the piazza's incessant tourist static to afford a measure of quiet. The Foundation's façade is unremarkable, its finish distinguishable from its abutting neighbors only by its reddish hue. What draws attention, oddly enough, is a handrail. To reach the foundation from the *campiello*, we must first cross the Rio Santa Maria Canal and, although two bridges present themselves (a curious doubling even at the entry), Scarpa's bridge beckons with its glistening teak rail. The rail seems suspended above the canal, the teak's fine grain a luminescent golden brown, a live thing amid all the gray stone and stucco. Scarpa has eccentrically configured the rail to the grasp and joined the teak with nautical brass fittings that provide both visual and tactile accents; the brass, more than the wood, conducts the varying temperatures of the air. With great courtesy, then, Scarpa takes us by the hand.

The bridge's double now reveals itself as an ugly twin. Its stone undercarriage, sluggish pavers, and marble balustrade are no match for Scarpa's more Asian fabrication of arched steel and larchwood treads. The ugly twin is of the common Venetian type and dutifully maintains the fiction of the campo's solidity. Scarpa's bridge, on the other hand, serves notice with sound and sight: the softer thud of shoes on wood and the flicker of reflected light through spaced treads. The rail nudges again. We trace its trajectory from teak to steel strut, to steel support, to a second strut, to that strut's doubling. Each transition articulates a fundamental of structure: the negotiation of load to support, the translation of horizontal to vertical. Yet at the final critical connection of strut to bridge, there is nothing; the double struts simply fold and disappear into the span's plating, where steel abandons all skeletal pretense in a series of ductile laminations. Steel, we know, pours in a molten state during its manufacture, but it is rarely detailed with such liquid nonchalance. A bit of a trickster, this last joint, undermining habit like Shakespeare's fool: demanding attention and then retreating in a rush of gibberishness and a parting joke.

However, something stranger is happening. The bridge is eccentric; its crest is called out by an elliptical pin joint, the campo elevation clearly higher than our destination. Scarpa has subtly undercut this difference by eliding the connection of stone to steel, pulling up the campo border with Istrian steps rather than cleanly breaking to steel at the campo. The destination is stranger still: it is a window (not a door) through a wall (which is disintegrating) into what is clearly the basement of the palazzo. And the window frame, which we slam up against, has a double door in it. These doors reintroduce steel, but in a different guise: cold, heavy, rusted stock is woven and grommeted with a penal vengeance. The doors pinch us, yank us inward, and clang shut. With this sudden acceleration of effects, we are inside.

"As for the cellar," writes Gaston Bachelard, "we shall no doubt find uses for it. It will be rationalized and its conveniences enumerated. But it is first and foremost the *dark entity* of the house, the one that partakes of subterranean forces. When we dream there, we are in harmony with the irrationality of the depths." Bachelard obviously wrote in the comfort of a well-lit second-floor study, for the foyer of the Querini Stampalia Foundation is a difficult space to harmonize with, thwarting, as it does, every expectation. The low foyer counters the expanse of the bridge with an abrupt compression. The ceiling is finished with de Luigi's luminescent *stucco lucido*, its reddish-brown pigments emanating from deep within successive plaster coats and reinforcing a subterranean mood. The wall's hovering plaster panels seem oblivious; their joints are at midwall and obscure the corners as if the space were continuous. Lacking the luster of their horizontal

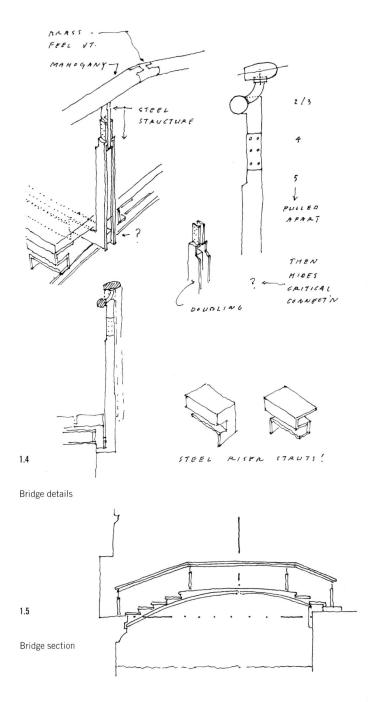

BRASS –
FEEL VT.

MAHOGANY

STEEL
STRUCTURE

2 / 3

4

5

PULLED
APART

← ?

THEN
HIDES
? ← CRITICAL
CONNECT'N

DOUBLING

1.4

STEEL RISER STRUTS !

Bridge details

1.5

Bridge section

cousin, the wall's plaster finish is the rumpled, dull gray of some unfortunate pachyderm—skin, it is clear from the water staining at the lower edges, that will eventually drop off.

Small canals run about the edges of the foyer floor and define it as a minicampo surrounded by waterways that protect it against the *acqua alta.* Elegant too are the marble tiles composed as an undifferentiated field in homage to the paintings of Josef Albers, much as the ceiling owes something to those of Mark Rothko. Yet the tile's reflective finish more vividly recalls the surface of water, and the configuration of campo and canal also suggests that of a pool. Does the foyer offer protection from the water or something more insidious? And what are we to make of the odd door, its brass cladding glowing across the foyer, its odd zigzag joint punctuated by eyelet fasteners? Again Scarpa engages us physically, testing our expectations, and we slowly discern the doors' folding mechanism and open its leaves, the light flashing and darting off its surfaces, to discover what treasure behind it?—an electrical closet.

Light streams from the honorific entryway just beyond the foyer portal. The portal itself is a succession of layers: stone, glass, plaster, concrete, and finally brick. Scarpa articulates every element of the palazzo's construction and history through slight misalignments and reveals, his respectful additions joining a conversation long in process. A brief respite, this elegant interlude.

Much as the foyer's campo suggested a square and then denied an easy centricity, the honorific entryway suggests an axis but then denies its potential symmetries. The axis misses the center of the distant doorway and dead-ends into the blank brick wall of the northeast room. True, there is a pairing of sorts between the transparencies of the gallery's glass partition wall and the water-gate's open grating, and between the little monument nested in the gallery glass wall and the potential human figure ascending the honorific stair from the canal. Again, the relationship does

1.6

Foyer

1.7

Foyer to porch

not reassure with symmetry but unsettles with strange twins. Materials reinforce these uncanny echoes: pedestrian concrete and Istrian stone are similar in material but different in appearance, while the reflective glass and luminous plaster are similar in appearance but different in material.

No restful composure exists between elements and, instead, a kind of jostling for position excites the space, a space that is deflecting outside to the canal and, grudgingly, inside to the gallery. The walls are left undressed, the yellow brick of the masonry structure scrubbed clean, while both the floor and the ceiling pull back, layer by layer, as they extend to the canal. The concrete floor is smooth, erratically marked with control joints and protected with a lip of Istrian stone, and it finally gives way to the cascade of the travertine treads that flow to the canal. Above, the ceiling's finish erodes to reveal its steel structure and scrap wood infill. Lights punctuate both exfoliations: the floor light accents the step to the gallery, while the ceiling fixture nests itself just as the shimmering plaster gives way to the flotsam and jetsam of wood. There is, again, an odd liquid quality to the detailing. The ceiling is water-stained and reflects a dappled light from the canal. The watergate's Byzantine tracery ripples and shimmers like windblown water, and it dissolves in brass accents and an intricate tripartite folding. The Istrian stone border zips and darts about—never accommodating the conventional break at the corners but winding through—leaving us to wonder, again, are we dry and safe on a pier, or have we mistakenly stepped into a water trough?

The odd little monument standing within the glass partition seems more intent on denying rather than asserting the solid geometries of its double-cube volume. Istrian stone reappears: gathering from column to kneewall to a lone figure, eroding to a void of dark glass, and returning to kneewall and column. Gold leaf inlay invites our fingers' trace, double squares appearing like a talisman, twice. The stone could be unfolded, it seems, as if

1.8

Porch from northeast room

the corners were inconsequential to its true fluid nature. Water is infectious: its ominous blue-green viscosity glimmers through the watergate and sucks at the stone steps. And make no mistake, we smell the water; an odoriferous effluvium assaults the space.

Straight ahead lies the shelter of the northeast room. As our eyes adjust to the dank darkness, however, it becomes apparent that there will be no refuge from the water. The ceiling's heavy steel beams lumber above, interlaced with a dark mold-green stucco. The wall's plaster panels dissipate to brick as Ionic columns sink into a drainage trough. Again, the floor is detailed for floods and its four-square scoring completes the room, in spite of the walls, somewhere in the canal outside. A little stair drops to the floor, its stone trim a fluid extension of the pier's stone border. The stair is rarely used. Instead, most people turn back, retrace their steps, pass around the monument and through the adjoining glass partition to arrive in the gallery.

Here, finally, there is a clarity of space and lack of agitation in the detailing. There is a quiet and a pause. The smell of the canal, at least, is not as pungent. The building no longer seems to have lost its will to decay and exfoliation for here are solid walls with a reassuring firmness. Just ahead, through the gallery's glass wall, is a garden. A gentle mound of grass, green blades rise to the sun in this city of dead stone pavers, fetid water, and decaying buildings. The way is clear; it is straight ahead. We simply walk between the columns.

Which columns? There are three pairs: the Ionic, the modern, and the ghosts of etched glass. None align. No matter, the water is behind us. Of course, we stepped down on our way into the gallery— not a good sign—and the floor wraps the sides of the wall to establish a waterline. So we are up to our ankles. The grass outside is above this line, but no matter, the water rises to our shins. The travertine will protect; its brass picture rail must establish a line of sight protected and secure.

1.9

Gallery to garden

Until we turn in doubt. Amid the blaze of reflections, as the building disintegrates in harsh light, we see that the brass rail is aligned with the crest of the bridge while the bridge rail aligns with the ceiling. We see that the precious monument was just a screen for a radiator whose hard snout pokes out. We remember that we last saw the travertine as pavers leading up from the canal (what is it doing here?) and remember that travertine is the residue of hot water, laden with minerals, that is forced out of the earth under pressure, then evaporates, leaving behind deposits of calcium carbonate. Travertine is petrified water and looks like it. Scarpa, ever attentive, has cut the stone against the grain here, not with the grain, as with the pavers. We are not stepping on the stone anymore, but are captured within its depth. And that plaster ceiling, it was there all along, extending uninterrupted from the entry, its polished surface now animated by lights darting about like so many water bugs. We are in a space that replicates the dimensions of the canal we had crossed, and thought we had left behind. Like a hapless character in an Edgar Allan Poe short story, we are trapped in the sinking basement of a godforsaken palazzo with all its history, references, and stifling decay.

But the light is so beautiful; a golden luminescence pervades the space. There is a quiet now; we are not slamming through a window or dropping off a pier. Gone is the frenzied detailing and the theatricality of quick jabs and nightmarish tricks. It is quiet. The water is present, yes, but it is not close enough to terrify, just close enough to prick sensibilities awake. We can breathe and there seems to be time . . . just to swim for a while.

A strange buoyancy fills the space. The water that first terrified now gently lifts to the horizontal. The concrete flooring reveals its stone aggregate with a dimpled texture. Istrian stone smoothly measures the concrete with a wavy syncopation down the length of the gallery, and the center strips run counter to this rhythm, sug-gesting a way for us to swim slowly forward, wandering. We roll,

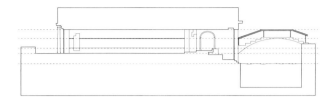

1.10

Gallery horizontal datum lines: canal
water, gallery floor, concrete revetment,
picture rail and bridge crest, gallery
ceiling and bridge rail

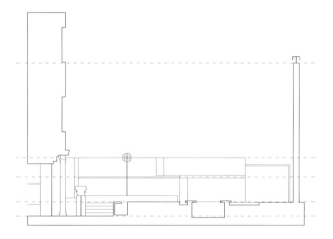

1.11

Garden horizontal datum lines:
gallery floor, lawn, glass tile in
concrete wall, top of concrete
wall, top of garden wall

expert swimmers, shoulders not locked parallel to the earth, but rotating from side to side. We let go of the earth.

For the floor is not just a floor, but laps up the wall. The joint from horizontal to vertical is unmarked, the Istrian stone transforms into a limpid light within the travertine, and the travertine's creamy grain runs horizontal and then vertical. The grain is never insistent, but rolls and floats up and down, forward and back. Even the brass rail seems to flicker somewhere between floor and ceiling, and to vanish unanswered and forgotten in the garden. For the space, in spite of its rectangular configuration, denies the insistence of perspective; no answering garden marker locks lines of sight into focus. Instead, the garden presents an empty field of green; a strange unanchored earth drifts and floats dreamily.

And there is a murmuring, a low hum, a sympathy between things. Scarpa's Istrian columns turn and nod to one another, one with its golden band and the other with its aquatic light. The columns defer to their Ionic elders and respectfully mark intervals of the half and the third, a gentle play that the etched glass joins. The reflection of the distant watergate appears like a benevolent ghost who suggests that the way out is not easy or clear or, in the end, so pressing. Our gaze drifts to the periphery for, again, there is no center, just a drifting field of green. A second radiator appears and is animated by another aspect: its iron body is hunkered into a crouch like the lion of St. Mark in the garden beyond—neither set to pounce and dominate with the positivistic rhetoric of technology, nor ironic, joking at its own feebleness and the unknowable transience of the past. A quiet sympathy, then: laying low, purring, nodding to stories.

For they have several stories to tell, the lion laden with iconographic significance here in Venice much as the radiator, in the legacy of modernism, has had its reign. And they both look to the

Corinthian capital, the ruffled mane of the lion and the crenella-
tions of the radiator finding a sympathetic ornamentation in the
capital's foliation. Foliation now reassures us against the decayed
exfoliations of the entry sequence. These fragments are not fragments at all in the sense that fragments are an elegiac reference to
a single, now lost, unity. Capital, lion, and radiator are, more accurately, figures. There is no totalizing scheme, no one direction;
there are only figures with their own resonance suggesting many
narratives, movements, and discoveries. And let us be clear about
this: I am telling only one story, and I am telling it on a good day.

However, Scarpa seems to me to be not only intelligent and mas-
terful in his architecture, but generous and gracious as well. For he
cannot resist it: as we drift to the glass wall and discover that there
are three exits (more than enough), Scarpa offers a final figure.
The wall that appeared monolithic holds a little door. The door,
its travertine grain swirling about and its sill slipping up the
jambs, opens with a nudge to reveal a second little gallery. It is a
gentle reminder to pay attention, especially to distractions.

Finally, we are outside, in the garden. We come into the sunlight
and the smell of grass, ivy, linden, and cherry trees. This garden
is not contained so much as wrapped by layers of ivy-draped
brick, concrete, and plaster, each slipping about the next without
closing at the corners. Again, the center is left vacant, the green
island circumnavigated by a school of smaller, peripheral embellishments. We discover these embellishments in a circuitous
manner: going forward and back, circling the green island in a
maze of effects.

The same washed concrete flooring slips outside, guiding us
upright as if to step from the water. The Istrian banding of the
concrete also glides to the vertical in the quoining of the concrete
retaining wall, then springs to life in the flowering of the Corinthian capital. A canal appears, but this time it is controlled: a miniature holding purer water dotted by green lilies, the water at waist

1.12

Garden to entry

1.13

Garden concrete screen wall
and bronze water tray

height, inviting a dip of the hand. The water's source is a labyrinth of luminescent alabaster, a miniature abstraction of Venice that hovers above the canal, its iconography answered at the far end by the lion of St. Mark. Sounds of water fill the space: the steady stream from the alabaster labyrinth, a gurgling from somewhere behind the lion, and two other barely perceptible splashings.

Just upstream, a light peers behind a small cherry tree, a small beacon slightly misaligned with the water channel. Successive washings of the screen wall's aggregate gauge our ascent even as the wall staggers away, refusing to solidify, as multicolored glass tiles mark the centerline of the concrete and undermine notions of above and below. Looking up to the top of the garden wall, we see an articulate steel rail of doubled hooks and circles (are there people up there, too?). Where is ground level after all, where is terra firma? Hard to tell. Instead, there is the strange sensation of hovering in a zone of water and sky as the earth drifts somewhere in the mix.

Even the walk's concrete retaining wall seems to return to its original viscous mix for its quoining doubles, triples, and finally, obscures its defining right angles. Water appears again, overflowing a bronzed metal tray of water lilies—lively green foliation everywhere now—the tray set into a tiled basin whose configuration and finish recall the foyer's campo. As is so often the case in Venice, there is an impasse, bounded by water, the concrete screen wall, and the hedge of hydrangea. We must double back, and we discover an odd little stair tucked against the entry colonnade. The stair literally steps, the hollow metal percussion of the steel treads announcing our trespass into the service zone of the garden— a zone that, in most architectural strategies, would be inviolate or, at the least, unpleasant.

Instead, we find a third water feature hidden behind the lion and a clump of pittosporum. The canal channels into a small steel scupper, a scupper we can adjust to modulate the flow and sound

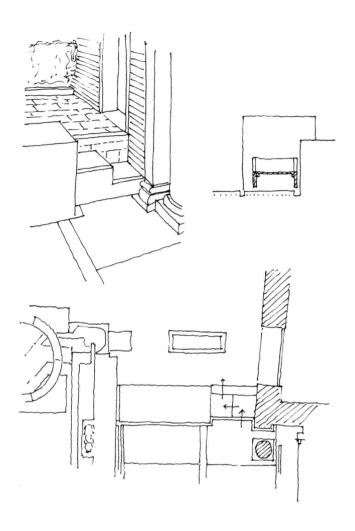

1.14

Colonnade steps

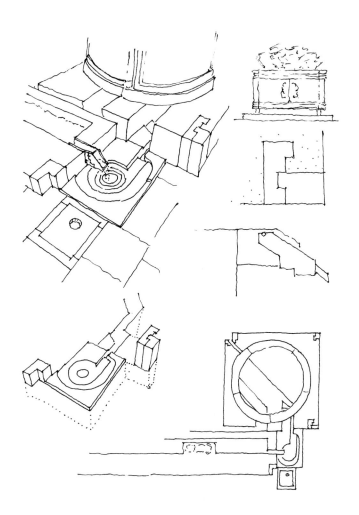

1.15

Well, scupper, and quoining

of the water. The water empties into a swirling pool of marble, ducks into the cleft of a miniature concrete plinth, and vanishes beneath a fifteenth-century marble well enclosure that hovers above (an odd cistern, this one). The concrete and stone liquefy; their joints recede in darkness and an Istrian doubling obfuscates their defining corners. This same stonework dives into the marble basin to resurface as a doubling on the far corner, the Japanese model of wooden joinery translated into a strange fluid geology. A kind of minisublime pours into a fresh aquatic perception of the physical world.

Across the lawn, the concrete screen wall reveals a split. We pass a wooden door to the alley, a stout grid of larchwood strips with an elongated steel hinge that announces its pivoting operation. Wood joins the catalog of doors: steel, brass, iron, stone, and glass. Yet if doors, as Georg Simmel writes, offer "the possibility at any moment of stepping out of . . . limitation into freedom," a locked door suggests the opposite. Scarpa, after all, has choreographed this walk in the manner of a cloister, a perambulation about an inviolate center. In many ways, the garden perimeter is the benevolent twin of the entry, which is itself a kind of ecclesiastical porch. The garden's deliberate sequence of aquatic effects underscores nature's salubrious potential, while the porch surrenders to nature's entropic demons. And the gallery, it is true, is a kind of nave that negotiates between the two or, in a more optimistic vein, delivers us from one world to the next. Scarpa has drawn us in as unwitting novices to a stern pantheistic order. However, in this catechism, we advance by violating rather than obeying boundaries.

Just beyond the door, a path of concrete pavers skirts the garden wall. The pavers nest in the grass like so many stepping-stones, and it seems appropriate to unlace our shoes, just in case. The pavers match the sway of our hips and shoulders and vanish into the far, low concrete wall, which folds to allow the trayed pond

1.16

Basin in potting yard

1.17

Aerial view of garden

to continue as a canal. And there is yet another sound, a trickle. Winding behind the wall, or wading in the channel as if in some benevolent dream of the *acqua alta*, we come upon a thin sheet of water that drops from a small stone channel into a shallow basin not more than a foot in diameter, and then disappears as if to the source of the garden's liquid symphony. Now in the potting yard of the garden, clearly out of bounds, we must kneel to discern this final waterwork. An invitation to splash our face and drink this clear, pure water.

The pressure of the wall and the open phrasing of the pavers invite a final trespass onto the grass. The lawn has no overriding geometry, and no axes command obedience. Instead, the lawn suggests an endless series of double squares that ripple and flicker, teasing out an infinite number of associations among well, light, canal, lion, door, island, maze, fountain, and font. All these events occur on the periphery, the central space we occupy only now, almost as an afterthought.

———

But enough of associations as if architecture were only a text to be read. And, for that matter, enough of precious effects as if architecture were only a succession of discrete contrivances. Wonderful as these effects are, they remain aloof, objectlike, inviting cerebral appreciation and tactile participation without combining to create an enveloping ambient affect. What of the space? If the frantic theatricality of the entry sequence releases to the spatial affect of the gallery—the wonderful luxurious swim— does the cloister's sometimes cloying parade of waterworks set up a similar affect in the garden?

Certainly, the incessant cacophony of details now recedes into the background, either muffled behind screen walls and planting or set below the line of sight. The effects that remain are subdued: the touch of cool grass, the scent of cherry trees, the sound of running water, the wrap of ivy on brick, the sky above. Control loosens; cultivation yields. Slight trees and shrubs root into a homogenous field of grass that surrenders to the encroachment of ivy. We stand, yes, but on a strange floating earth that folds to the vertical in a blanket of verdure, a blanket that blurs defining corners and edges. The gallery tilted us to the horizontal to swim to the island of grass and, having finally reached the island, it, too, folds and releases us into the deep field of the sky. We have been lured out of bounds into a liminal state, where primal orientations of up and down are destabilized, and we now float suspended, wrapped in a green cloak that finally, simply, lets go.

But why the recapitulation, why the return to bibelots? Why not cut straight to the lawn? Even in Italy where we seldom walk on grass, there must be a more direct route. Several reasons suggest themselves: Scarpa's affinity with objects lent itself to construction detailing, and the scarcity of commissions curtailed his spatial explorations; Scarpa's devout Catholicism reinforced the narrative possibilities of architecture; and, certainly, the repeated Venetian floods would reinforce in anyone the desire to grab onto solid things. Scarpa's details repeatedly elicit a tactile response to materials even as those materials seem to dissolve.

I myself am torn. The garden perimeter sometimes seems an unnecessary profusion of melodies and, at other times, a necessary bridge to the final coda of the lawn. Late in his career, Scarpa himself would sometimes dismiss his details as "scarpini," as if they were the first expression of his liquid architecture and he recognized that he must suppress them to realize the full affect of his unique aquatic sensibility. Tragically, just as his career was gaining momentum, Scarpa died. He rests in what he considered his masterpiece, the Brion Cemetery. At his request, Scarpa is interred in the manner of a medieval knight: wrapped in a white cloak, upright, perpendicular to the earth.

Bibliographic Notes

"Swimming at the Querini Stampalia Foundation" initiated this series of essays, and, with it, I developed a method that I followed with its successors. Every essay was precipitated by a building visit, one that startled me. I grew up on a dairy farm where constructing was as regular as milking cows, and I am now a practicing architect who teaches design and construction in the university. It is not surprising, therefore, that what often startled me was unorthodox construction, construction that seemed to infect the surrounding spaces. After my initial visit, I read the available critical and historical commentary, all the while revisiting the building, so that I could measure the understandings of others against my own experience. If I remained flummoxed, as I was by all four of these buildings, I began to write. I wrote from memory, gradually translating construction and space into words through an imaginative act that allowed me to navigate these strange territories. Because I think of my essays as the products of informed imagination rather than rigorous scholarship, I have dispensed with conventional footnotes. Instead, I close each essay by crediting the scholarship that was directly relevant, useful, or inspiring to me during my writing. Other writers may have proposed interpretations similar to my own, but unless otherwise indicated I arrived at them on my own.

Two historians provided a foundation for all my essays. Edward R. Ford meticulously documented the construction strategies of canonical architects in the two volumes of *The Details of Modern Architecture*, and Kenneth Frampton outlined the development of modern building technologies within a broad cultural context in his encyclopedic *Studies in Tectonic Culture*. My understandings of

individual buildings differ from Ford's refined modernist predilec-
tions and Frampton's learned deferrals to Semper, Heidegger, and
Marx; however, I enjoy the combined luxury of their scholarship
and a narrower focus.

My treatment of the Querini Stampalia Foundation is indebted
to Manfredo Tafuri's essay "Carlo Scarpa and Italian Architecture"
in *Carlo Scarpa, The Complete Works*. Tafuri describes Scarpa's
propensity for "erosion and fluidification" (85) and his "doubling
of elements" (86). He distinguishes the term "fragment" as it is
deployed by Scarpa's critics, most notably Francesco Dal Co in his
essay "The Architecture of Carlo Scarpa" (27), from the more
helpful term "figure" (86); I make use of all these observations.
However, Tafuri argues that Scarpa is primarily a writer of architectural texts—texts that are open to interpretation in the manner
of Umberto Eco, but texts that Tafuri's Marxist proclivities lead
him, finally and somewhat dismissively, to characterize as "infinite
entertainment" (95). While acknowledging Scarpa's myriad res-
onances, my understanding of the Querini Stampalia Foundation
is more akin to that which Henri Lefebvre advocates in *The Production of Space*: "What we are concerned with here is not texts but
texture" (222). For me, Scarpa's work truly opens when he dis-
cards architectural associations for a more comprehensive spatial engagement.

Also in *Carlo Scarpa, The Complete Works* is "The Life of Carlo
Scarpa" by Giuseppe Mazzariol and Giuseppe Barbieri, which I depended upon for biographical information. My account of Scarpa's
burial comes from this essay (22) as does the parallel between
Venice's geology and glass's composition (13). My overview of
Venice's history and the construction of its campos and palaces is
based on Richard J. Goy's *Venice*, Deborah Howard's *An Architectural History of Venice*, and *Knopf Guide* (this last book is particularly valuable for its illustrations of Venice). I turned to Richard

Murphy's *Querini Stampalia Foundation* for specifics of the Querini Stampalia's history and construction, and have cited his accounts of Le Corbusier's visit (3), the persistence of Venetian craft (7), Scarpa's working method (9), the influence of Albers (9), and the Foundation's mission (10).

Scarpa's apocryphal description of the Venetian floods is from Manlio Brusatin's "The Architect in Asolo" (195), and the source for Scarpa's curious genealogical assertion is Giuseppe Zambonini's "Process and Theme in the Work of Carlo Scarpa" (22). Zambonini also asserts that "all the samples prepared by his lifetime friend and executor of plaster work, Mario de Luigi, were derived from a book on the painter, Mark Rothko" (28). My description of the effects of Scarpa's glasswork is my own, but my account of Scarpa's development of glasswork techniques is based on "Glassware" by Attilia Dorigato (183–185) and Mary Plant's descriptions in *Venice, Fragile City* (307–320). Mildred Friedman offers a more comprehensive history of Scarpa's American proponents in her essay "Scarpa Today."

The remaining quotations are from the works of philosophers and critics: Martin Heidegger's definition of building is from "Building, Dwelling, Thinking" (146), and his description of the Greek temple comes from "The Origin of the Work of Art" (42); the Gaston Bachelard passage is from *The Poetics of Space* (18); and the Georg Simmel passage is from "Bridge and Door" (10).

Finally, I offer a caveat. In my account of the Querini Stampalia Foundation, I emphasize that "I am telling only one story, and I am telling it on a good day." However, if we recognize our ecological predicament in Scarpa's Venice, which I think we must, and if Scarpa envisioned redemption in the garden of the Querini Stampalia Foundation, which I think he did, we should be aware that Scarpa did so on the strength of his Catholic faith rather than by a rigorous assessment of the facts.

Bibliography

Bachelard, Gaston. *The Poetics of Space*, trans. Maria Jolas. Boston: Beacon Press, 1969.

Brusatin, Manlio. "The Architect in Asolo." In *Carlo Scarpa, The Complete Works*, ed. Francesco Dal Co and Giuseppe Mazzariol, trans. Richard Sadleir, 195–197. New York: Electa/Rizzoli, 1985, © 1984.

Dal Co, Francesco. "The Architecture of Carlo Scarpa." In *Carlo Scarpa, The Complete Works*, ed. Francesco Dal Co and Giuseppe Mazzariol, trans. Richard Sadleir, 24–71. New York: Electa/Rizzoli, 1985, © 1984.

Dorigato, Attilia. "Glassware." In *Carlo Scarpa, The Complete Works*, ed. Francesco Dal Co and Giuseppe Mazzariol, trans. Richard Sadleir, 183–185. New York: Electa/Rizzoli, 1985, © 1984.

Ford, Edward R. "The Venturis, Graves, Scarpa, and the Layers of History: 1963–1984." In *The Details of Modern Architecture, Volume 2: 1928–1988*, 349–377. Cambridge, MA: The MIT Press, 1996.

Frampton, Kenneth. "Carlo Scarpa and the Adoration of the Joint." In *Studies in Tectonic Culture: The Poetics of Construction in Nineteenth and Twentieth Century Architecture*, ed. John Cava, 299–333. Cambridge, MA: The MIT Press, 1995.

Frampton, Kenneth. "Introduction: Reflections on the Scope of the Tectonic." In *Studies in Tectonic Culture: The Poetics of Construction in Nineteenth and Twentieth Century Architecture*, ed. John Cava, 1–28. Cambridge, MA: The MIT Press, 1995.

Friedman, Mildred. "Scarpa Today." In *Carlo Scarpa Architect, Intervening with History*, ed. Nicholas Olsberg and Mildred Friedman, 237–247. New York: The Monacelli Press, and Montreal: Canadian Centre for Architecture, 1999

Goy, Richard J. *Venice: The City and Its Architecture*. London: Phaidon Press, 1997.

Heidegger, Martin. "Building, Dwelling, Thinking." In *Poetry, Language, Thought*, trans. Albert Hofstadter, 143–161. New York: Harper & Row, 1971.

Heidegger, Martin. "The Origin of the Work of Art." In *Poetry, Language, Thought*, trans. Albert Hofstadter, 15–87. New York: Harper & Row, 1971.

Howard, Deborah. *An Architectural History of Venice.* New Haven, CT: Yale University Press, 2002.

Knopf Guide. *Knopf Guide: Venice.* New York: Alfred A. Knopf, 1993.

Lefebvre, Henri. *The Production of Space,* trans. David Nicholson-Smith. London: Blackwell Publishers, 1991.

Mazzariol, Giuseppe, and Giuseppe Barbieri. "The Life of Carlo Scarpa." In *Carlo Scarpa, The Complete Works,* ed. Francesco Dal Co and Giuseppe Mazzariol, trans. Richard Sadleir, 9–23. New York: Electa/Rizzoli, 1985, © 1984.

Murphy, Richard. *Querini Stampalia Foundation.* London: Phaidon Press, 1993.

Plant, Mary. *Venice, Fragile City: 1797–1997.* New Haven, CT: Yale University Press, 2002.

Simmel, Georg. "Bridge and Door," trans. Mark Ritter. *Theory, Culture and Society* 11 (1994): 5–10.

Tafuri, Manfredo. "Carlo Scarpa and Italian Architecture." In *Carlo Scarpa, The Complete Works,* ed. Francesco Dal Co and Giuseppe Mazzariol, trans. Richard Sadleir, 72–96. New York: Electa/Rizzoli, 1985, © 1984.

Zambonini, Giuseppe. "Process and Theme in the Work of Carlo Scarpa." *Perspecta 20: The Architectural Journal* (1983): 21–42.

2.1

Jacobs House, view from garden

2 THE JACOBS HOUSE, BURNING FIELDS

In late 1927, Frank Lloyd Wright wrote his estranged son John Lloyd Wright with an invitation to rejoin his practice in Phoenix, Arizona. Extolling the potential of the burgeoning city—"This is a great region for a young man, it is going to be the playground of the United States soon"—the elder Wright also pledged a new diligence in meeting salary obligations, obligations that he had not met in the past and had led to the breach. John Lloyd appreciated the overture but declined the offer, knowing that his father's promise of fiscal responsibility was as bankable as his bold economic forecasts. A personal aside of his father did ring true, however, and John Lloyd was later to remark:

> *I wonder if when Dad wrote, 'Phoenix seems to be the name for me too . . . ,' he was likening himself to the bird of which there is only one of its kind alive at a time; the bird most celebrated of all the symbolic creatures fabricated by the ancient mysteries; the bird who consumes*

*itself with its own fire and then rises in youthful freshness
out of its own ashes.*

As John Lloyd's mythic imagery suggests, his father's allure
was still powerful even if his blandishments were ineffective. Yet
the simile is apt. When he wrote his son, Frank Lloyd Wright had
risen from the ashes. Wright had risen, by my count, for the sixth
time: (1) provincial Wisconsin escaped for the Chicago offices of
Adler and Sullivan; (2) dismissal for moonlighting countered with
the succor of family and independent practice in Oak Park; (3)
abandonment of family and practice for love affair with a client,
Margaret Borthwick Cheney, then a subsequent release to Europe
and the triumphant publication of the Wasmuth portfolio; (4)
holocaust at Spring Green consuming Cheney, children, and house
mitigated by the luxurious commission of the Imperial Hotel in
Tokyo; (5) entanglements with a second wife, Miriam Noel, flight
to Los Angeles, and a succession of inventive textile block commissions; and (6) second Spring Green fire coupled with the threat
of bank foreclosure that led, inevitably it seems by this time, to
a final resurgence. Egyptian cosmology aside, Wright seemed to
not avoid these conflagrations so much as test them for updraft.

Finally, in this Wright's sixth regeneration, something like
stability set in. But it was a stability with its own vicissitudes, vicissitudes brought on by forces outside Wright, most notably the
Great Depression and the Second World War, but also by Wright
himself—his inveterate cussedness and thirst for self-promotion
favoring a combination of the two. These singes aside, Wright's
final quarter-century generally followed the upward trajectory of
his native country as it, too, arose from economic ruin, galvanized
itself in battle, and shifted the world's attention and resources to
itself. Lofted by his enterprising young wife Olgivanna Milanov
Wright, liberated by the expanse of the southwestern desert, ac-
companied by an endless clutch of bright young apprentices,

and gathering winglike an encyclopedic range of architectural references, Wright took his final extended flight.

Wright gyred through the 1930s. He lectured extensively; he wrote an autobiography and three books on architecture (*Modern Architecture, Disappearing City,* and *Architecture and Modern Life* with Baker Brownell); he established a school at Spring Green with winter quarters outside Phoenix (the school's name, Taliesin, linking it with the Welsh myth of artistic rejuvenation); and he produced significant work in planning with Broadacre City, in commercial architecture with the S. C. Johnson and Son Administration Building, in academic architecture with Taliesin West and Florida Southern College, and in domestic architecture with the Edgar J. Kaufman House FallingWater—a house that elevated Wright, at the end of the decade, to a dedicated issue of *Architectural Forum,* the cover of *Time* magazine, and a retrospective at the Museum of Modern Art in New York City. Amid this flurry, Wright also designed a small house in Madison, Wisconsin, for a young couple, Herbert and Katherine Jacobs. Wright had produced canonical works of domestic architecture at the beginning of the century and, in 1936 at the age of sixty-nine, he reimagined the single-family house yet again. He did it in less than 1,500 square feet for a total cost of $5,500.

The Jacobs House's modest dimensions belie Wright's immodest aspirations. The house underpins Wright's utopian project "Usonia," his dream of a newly mobile American citizenry returning to Jeffersonian agrarianism with the family as the central benevolent social unit. Wright called forth his dream with Broadacre City: a four-square-mile settlement of 1,400 families wherein agriculture, light industry, and parks were interlaced with commercial, recreational, and civic buildings by networks for power, communication, and the automobile. The single-family Usonian House, the Jacobs House being the first built, was to be the module for this extended field.

John Lloyd Wright's pyric ruminations, however, intimate a fiercer conception of house, family, and landscape. Wright designed the Jacobs House during his most remarkable resurgence, yet it seems poised to move in the opposite direction, to the ashes. The Jacobs House, after all, is made of the most perishable of all building materials, wood, which Wright detailed with a disregard so meticulous that his attitude cannot be dismissed as cavalier.

———

Wright was devoted to the Jacobs House. The Jacobses themselves inspired Wright's devotion, at least in part. A journalist working during the Great Depression, Herbert Jacobs had limited financial resources. However, Herbert's interests were broad-ranging; he was a graduate of Harvard, and—more important to Wright who placed little value in formal education and less in that of the East Coast—he and Katherine were intrigued by Wright's architecture and were sympathetic to Wright's peculiar agrarian ideals. The Jacobses became such committed clients that they purchased a second, larger lot when it became apparent that Wright's expectations for the house exceeded their own. For his part, Wright was attentive to the Jacobses' needs and the demands of construction. Wright was firm in his assessment of the Jacobses' furnishings—"This stuff is all prehistoric and it will have to go"—but he accommodated his design to their growing family and welcomed their improvements in diffused lighting and ceiling treatment. Wright supervised much of the construction himself, culled bricks from the S. C. Johnson construction site for their use, paid for expensive redwood battens when the Jacobses could not afford them, and approached manufacturers to sponsor the experimental heating system.

Of course, Wright presented himself as a hard-nosed pragmatist. "To give the small Jacobs family the benefit of the advantages of the era in which they live," Wright explained in his book *The Natural House*:

> *Many simplifications must take place. Mr. and Mrs. Jacobs must themselves see life in somewhat simplified terms. What are essentials in their case, a typical case? It is not only necessary to get rid of all unnecessary complications in construction, necessary to use work in the mill to good advantage, necessary to eliminate, so far as possible, field labor which is always expensive: it is necessary to consolidate and simplify the three appurtenance systems—heating, lighting, and sanitation. At least this must be our economy if we are to achieve the sense of spaciousness and vista we desire in order to liberate the people living in the house.*

Wright had long railed against the academic flourishes of Beaux-Arts classicism; he now argued that his architecture was one of economic necessity, not simply stylistic preference, and that modern technologies afforded improvements that had been stifled by nostalgia for outmoded styles. Continuing, Wright asked, "Now what can be eliminated?" In his response, it is clear that Wright was attacking vernacular as well as academic conventions. Wright listed nine items, each one typical of standard residential construction: the pitched roof, the detached garage, the basement, interior trim, radiators and lighting fixtures, "furniture, pictures, and bric-a-brac," paint, plaster, and gutters and downspouts. Wright proposed a reconsideration of residential construction from top to bottom, inside to outside.

Depression-era house construction was not fundamentally different from what we now find in any number of residential developments throughout the United States. Currently identified in building codes as wood light frame construction, it is a simple and efficient package, one that has only marginally changed with the introduction of power tools, composite materials, discontinuous vertical members, and more aggressive systems of climate control. Indeed, wood light frame construction is so ubiquitous that we are oblivious to its remarkable effects. If we visit a construction site for the first time, however, one thing is apparent: this tenuous filigree of sticks does not look as if it will stand up so much as blow away were it not tethered to its foundation by the stringlike wisp of its chimney. Timber framers were introduced to the wood light frame over 150 years ago and, with great acuity, nicknamed it the "balloon frame."

The conflation of skin (balloon) and structure (frame) is particularly apt. Instead of being independent, as in braced timber construction and steel and concrete frame construction, a wood light frame and its plywood skin are interdependent, the sheathing providing lateral bracing for the knitting of lumber that would otherwise topple sideways like a drunk in a windstorm. And, while it is reasonable to assume that all perimeter walls in a wood light framed house are structural and that a quick look in the basement will indicate how interior loads are carried above, structural walls look no different from their nonstructural counterparts. Finally, building codes now mandate very conservative construction guidelines, but anyone who has renovated an old house appreciates how forgiving a wood light frame is to even the most optimistic structural calculations and inept craftsmanship. Any fool could build such a house and many fools did—the house, like an expert boxer, deflects and counters these bunglers but it rarely falls down.

This, therefore, is Wright's inheritance: an immanently pragmatic system of construction even if it does not look rational, and one that is resilient even if it looks as if it might blow away at any moment. Wright will fundamentally reconfigure this inheritance and push its temporal implications to the limit.

Excavators had an easy time of it at the Jacobs House, insofar as anything was easy during the Great Depression. The basement (dug by hand) is barely 125 square feet, just large enough to accommodate the furnace and communicating stair. A horse-drawn grader only scraped the remaining building footprint since the foundation is a thin concrete slab. Such foundations are cheap but are not usually seen in Wisconsin, at least not for any length of time, because moisture creeps under the slab, expands and contracts as it freezes and thaws, and spits the crumbling concrete out of the ground. Wright avoided this problem by using the system of an elder Welsh stonemason who had constructed foundations at the Wright compound in Spring Green. After skimming the site, the men dug a trench around the perimeter of the slab to a depth of eighteen inches, sloped it to drain, and filled it with rocks the size of a fist to direct moisture away from the house. The crew then poured a four-inch slab with thickened edges over a net of steel reinforcing, stained it red, trimmed it with a band of brick, and scored it with control joints that followed the 2 x 4-foot module of wood light frame construction. A foundation can anchor a building to its site empathetically as well as physically, an anchoring that Wright restated in the projecting base courses of his earlier Prairie houses. The foundation of the Jacobs House, however, is indifferent to this role; it drifts, carpetlike, on the ground's surface. Reinforcing this visual cue is a tactile one; the slab is warm even in the dead of winter.

While working on the Imperial Hotel in Japan, Wright was intrigued by the Korean technique of circulating hot air through the cavities of tile flooring, transforming the coldest part of the room into a giant radiator. Wright named this principle "gravity heat," in reference to the cycling of air, which rises when heated and sinks when cooled. At the Jacobs House, Wright instructed the contractor, P. B. Grove, to set a network of two-inch wrought iron pipe on a sand bed beneath the slab. Steam (and later, when steam proved ineffective, hot water) circulated through the now radiant slab. Gravity heat and radiant slabs have significant advantages over conventional systems. The gentle circulation of gravity heat eliminates the chilling drafts of forced air systems, and radiant slabs absorb the ungainly radiators of standard hot water systems (radiators that Wright screened in his Prairie houses). In addition, a radiant slab convects heat throughout the physical body of the house, making surfaces warm to the touch, and heats the human body similarly by starting at the coldest extremity, the feet.

Wright combined gravity heat with two, even cheaper energy sources: the wind and sun. The Jacobs House turns its back to both the frigid northern winter winds and the scorching western summer sun. In the summer, the house's glazed garden walls open to accept breezes that cool as they drift across the concrete slab, which is shaded by generous roof overhangs, while warmer air rises and exhausts out the clerestory windows. In the winter, with the sun lower on the horizon, the sun reaches deep within the house, warming the slab and adding to its radiant heat. We often equate comfort with temperature and ignore the effects of drafts and radiating surfaces. Katherine Jacobs, however, discovered that her house was as comfortable in the winter as a conventional house that was ten degrees warmer. The slab feels and looks like a warm red rug.

What the foundation loses in chthonic power, the fireplace and chimney gain with authority. Fireplaces had long lost their functional role when Wright designed his Prairie houses and, as Vincent Scully has recounted, resurrected the fireplace as a symbolic center for the family and as a formal device to pin the houses' crossing volumes to their sites. The fireplace arrives at the Jacobs House with reinforcements, its brick mass swelling to include the kitchen and bathroom. Congruent with the slab, the bricks gradually heat during the winter and cool during the summer, their mass stabilizing temperatures within the house. As the only element that extends above the roof, the brick core also exhausts heat and odors from the kitchen and bathroom. Massive, with recessed skylights, the core is the only part of the house that extends below grade; the basement mechanical room rests below.

Two masonry fragments break away from the core. One extends to the south, bracketing the living area, and a second extends to the west, supporting the carport roof. Wright's strategy, in keeping with his goal of mass-producing Usonian houses, was to "bring the factory to the site": span the roof between masonry piers and provide Grove with a protected area for his wood shop. Although Grove was eager to build the Jacobs House, and the house testifies to his diligence and ingenuity, Herbert Jacobs reported that contractor and architect did not agree on this point: "'Build the roof first, and put the house under it,' Wright had suggested earlier, but Grove thought he was joking and proceeded in the conventional way, putting up the walls first." Grove's doubts were reasonable; the roof bears on the wood walls. Nevertheless, we will dutifully follow Wright to the roof and then catch up with Grove at the walls.

Having fulfilled his promise to eliminate the basement, radiators, and detached garage, Wright moved to the pitched roof and its unsightly battery of gutters and downspouts. Wright did this with great verve, the culmination of a career during which he had scrambled up the gable like Buster Keaton, stood triumphant on its peak, and, in a series of acrobatic jumps, flattened it. Wright's family house in Oak Park featured a prominent gable, his Prairie houses tamped the gable into a subdued hip roof, and his California houses pounded the roof below the parapet. At the Jacobs House, Wright flattened the roof from above and below, compressing it into a thin wafer.

Yet here again, visual effect combines with economic frugality. Although typically referred to as "flat," the roofs have a slope sufficient to direct rainwater and melting snow to perimeter drains hidden within the generous overhangs—no more gutters and downspouts. Spanning in a straight line what a pitched roof must triangulate, the roofs require less material while maintaining adequate space for insulation and ventilation. Finally, Wright eliminated the attic, which in his estimation was nothing more than a dustbin for middle-class clutter.

The roofs look simple in construction—How difficult can a flat plane be?—but they are not. Budget constraints ruled against the expense of the 2 x 12 rafters that the spans required, and, with typical aplomb, Wright argued that three 2 x 4's were cheaper than one 2 x 12 (which was true), that they would have the same depth if they were stacked one on top of the other (which was nearly true), and that they would also have the same strength (which was not true, but only evidently false when the roof sagged in later years). Chicanery aside, the roof is a woven structure of 2 x 4's. Furthermore, this woven structure allows for both the insertion of shims, so that the roof deck is sloped, and the staggering of fascia boards, so that the roof appears even thinner. Particularly in direct sunlight with the lower layers cast in shadow, the roofs seem anorexic. While a conventional gable acts as a counterpoint to the ground plane and asserts the house as a discreet object, and Wright's Prairie houses' demure hip roofs balance this assertion with a sympathetic recapitulation of the ground plane, the roof of the Jacobs House is so uncannily thin that it no longer echoes the ground. It evaporates on the ground's surface.

Historians have argued that elements of the International Style had crept into Wright's work by this time. Wright's resurgence in the 1930s was, without a doubt, fueled by his desire to reclaim modern architecture from a younger generation of Europeans who Wright believed (and, again, historians generally concur) stole it from him in the first place. In particular, after The International Style exhibition of 1932 at the Museum of Modern Art in New York City, Wright singled out Le Corbusier as the primary usurper. Wright's later work, at least in part, competed with that of Le Corbusier: Broadacre City was his reply to Le Corbusier's Plan Voisin, FallingWater was his response to Le Corbusier's Villa Savoye, and the Usonian houses were his alternative to Le Corbusier's Citrohan model for moderate-income housing. In 1928, Wright reviewed Le Corbusier's *Towards a New Architecture* with measured sympathy, but by the 1930s Wright could only accept Le Corbusier as a foil for his own concerns, and the exchange of ideas degenerated into transatlantic trash-talking: Wright dismissed Le Corbusier as "the Swiss discoverer," and Le Corbusier snapped back at Wright calling him "the blue-eyed prairie dog."

If Wright treated Le Corbusier as an upstart to be swatted early and often, Wright's relationship to another European architect who emerged from The International Style exhibition, Ludwig Mies van der Rohe, was more complex. Throughout his life, Mies was gracious in acknowledging the importance of Wright's early work, and, on his first trip to the United States in the summer of 1937, he visited Wright at Spring Green for an extended weekend that was, by all reports, a cordial interlude. Although we might attribute this easy rapport to Wright's loquaciousness and Mies's halting English, Wright and Mies seemed to have respected each other. This unusual sympathy ran deep: the massing of Mies's early projects resonated with Wright's work in Oak Park, and, later, Wright's building vocabulary echoed that of Mies. In particular, the Jacobs House's flat roof and wall configuration are familiar to anyone who has seen Mies's Barcelona Pavilion; Wright certainly had, because the pavilion was featured in The International Style exhibition. That architects might share a common vocabulary and steal from one another across distance and time is not, however, much of a revelation. To paraphrase T. S. Eliot: culture depends on theft. Nor should we be affronted by the desire to conceal these thefts, thefts that often come at great personal cost. That architects steal is far less revealing than how they steal. Wright's roof and wall are different from those of his contemporaries: they look different, they feel different, and, in a fundamental material sense, they are different.

Grove waits with the walls. And what odd walls they are. Wood light frame of a sort, being made of wood and undeniably light but—this must have given Grove pause—there is no frame. There are no studs, plates, headers, or sills. Wright pressed the frame into the skin so that they became one and the same. Vertical pine boards were sheathed with vapor-lock building paper and clad, again on both sides, with alternating horizontal bands of narrow $3\frac{1}{4}$-inch redwood battens and wide $9\frac{1}{2}$-inch pine boards. Brass screws, uniformly spaced and meticulously aligned to the horizontal, fastened the cedar battens to the core boards; the interlocking tongues and grooves fixed the unattached pine boards in place and allowed them to expand and contract with changes in temperature and moisture. Doors and windows were integral to this woven fabric; their casings were untrimmed and followed the regular interval of the slab's 2 x 4-foot grid. Indeed, Grove had another surprise: the slab was the drawing. The construction drawings of the Jacobs House were scored with the slab's grid but had no dimensions, so Grove's only alternative was to locate the wall configurations using the slab, much as he relied on the 13-inch vertical module of boards and battens to determine the wall heights. Wright had used horizontal boards and battens on a wood light frame as early as 1902 for the Gerts Cottage, and he may have seen a board and batten sandwich wall in the apple pickers' camps while working for the Bitter Root Valley Irrigation Company in Montana—he certainly tested the wall at the first Taliesin encampment, Ocotillo, outside Phoenix. Whatever its genesis, we are now

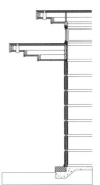

2.2

Jacobs House, wall section

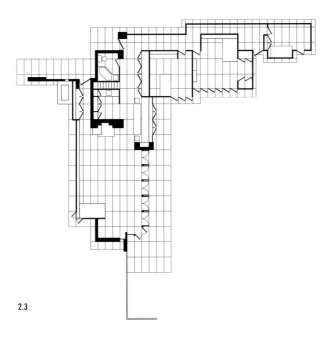

2.3

Jacobs House

faced with a wall barely 2½ inches thick and, we cannot help but note, with questionable insulating and structural properties.

Although this sandwich wall does not meet today's insulating standards, it exceeded the performance of its contemporaries. At the time, framed walls were rarely insulated and quickly became cold to the touch, for the vacant pockets between studs convected the frigid Wisconsin air. The sandwich wall squeezed out these pockets and, as we noted earlier, the wall convected the radiant slab's heat. In addition, air infiltration around doors and windows, a primary source of heat loss in conventional construction, decreased in the sandwich wall because the openings are integral to, rather than added to, the system. The structural integrity of the wall, on the other hand, was supplemented by the stabilizing mass of its brick counterparts, the regular folding of the wall itself, and, along uninterrupted lengths, the reinforcement of bookshelves mounted to the inside battens.

Perceptually, however, the wall seems insubstantial. Testing the wall with our knuckles, we do not get a reassuring thump but a feeble, high-pitched tap. Looking about, the windows do not appear to be openings punched in a stout enclosure so much as the acknowledgment of the enclosure's threadbare ephemerality. If the masonry core can be seen as Wright's version of the man-mountain of the Pueblo Indians, then we are now presented with its nomadic Amerindian opposite: the tent. Or, recalling another American vernacular, we can detect the ghost of a frontier cabin's logs and chinks in the banding of the Jacobs House's boards and battens. Yet here, too, the precedent is flattened, compressed, thin.

Within the context of modern architecture, this wall is more bizarre. At the time, Wright's European counterparts advocated a thin, nonbearing wall to distinguish it from a separate structural frame, but routinely built their wall as a thick impasto of stuccoed masonry. Wright, on the other hand, insisted on an organic unity that combined wall and structure, but in such a way that neither is believable. That is, Europeans built a nonbearing wall that looks structural, while Wright built a bearing wall that looks nonstructural. As Grove knew, most of the roof rafters at the Jacobs House bore directly on the walls below and often used the window and door casings as a crutch; hence, his incredulity at Wright's directive to build the roof first. Seeking out the walls' critical joints, we discover that there is no additional structure at the corners, the horizontal boards and battens run continuously with beveled edges, while the tops are casually tacked to the rafters and the bases are perched on a V-shaped zinc strip cast into the concrete slab. Wright's apprentices detailed everything with exquisite care, and Grove followed their directions with the precision of a cabinetmaker. Yet we, too, think Wright must be joking.

———

Strange humors inhabit the plan as well. At first glance, the plan seems stable enough being organized like the letter L: the brick core pinning the joint, the bedrooms and a study extending to the east, and a large living area extending to the south. An L is a common plan organization and is particularly effective for maintaining the edge of a corner site while protecting a private space behind. Wright exploited this strength: the outer walls of the Jacobs House brace the street with foreboding bands of board and brick that are only relieved by an upper clerestory and a flickering of glass at the entry, while the garden walls swing open with banks of glazed doors. Having set up this stable form, however, Wright sent it into a gentle spin, nudging it with the automobile. Wright's replacement for the detached garage, the carport, flies off the brick core to the west, opposing the garden on the diagonal, and its supporting walls stagger just enough to pinwheel the plan. The house no longer sets up the L's simple oppositions of public/private, bedroom/living room, street/garden, outside/inside, but is now defined as a more complex set of quadrants—front yard, garage, side yard, and garden—that refer to one another in a more varied and subtle conversation. The front yard and the side yard, for example, have more in common with each other than with the garden but are separated, nevertheless, by the carport and their own discrete characters.

Jump-starting the spin, Wright entered the house on the diagonal rather than in a more passive position, centered along the face of one of the legs. Wright loved automobiles, his passion for fast red roadsters leading to imprudent expenditures at Madison dealerships and impromptu sprints across the desert flats of Arizona, and, on a more prosaic level, he understood that people entered their houses from their automobiles and no longer promenaded up the front walk. By popping the walls off the traditional garage and cantilevering its now flat, flying roof, Wright created a generous portico, a grand entrance for a modest house. Looking beneath, however, we are baffled to discover not one but two doors.

The entry to the Jacobs House presented Wright with two problems. First, how could he provide a ceremonial entry and hide the detritus of family life? Second, how could he circulate through the house after having located the masonry core and the entrance in the same place? Taliesin histories abound with stories of Wright "shaking designs out of his sleeve," his uncanny ability to complete a design in one sitting. Although Wright's extraordinary facility is unquestionable, it is also true that he was an early riser and worked alone in his quarters before appearing in the drafting room, or, if inspiration struck early, awakening his beleaguered head draftsman John Howe to draw up an idea. Wright may have shaken designs out of his sleeve, but, like any magician, he made sure to stuff his sleeve first.

The design process of the Jacobs House is more accurately described in Wright's *An Autobiography*: "Now comes to brood—to

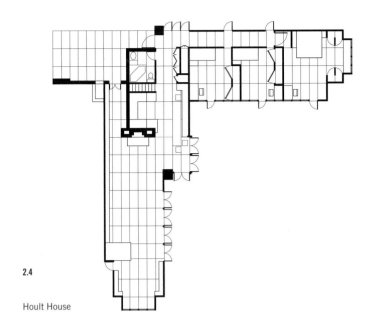

2.4

Hoult House

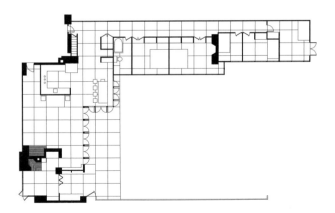

2.5

Lusk House

suffer doubt and burn with eagerness. To test bearings—and prove assumed ground by putting all together to definite scale on paper." When Wright accepted the Jacobs House commission, he had already tested bearings twice: first for the Hoult family in Wichita, Kansas, and second for the Lusk family in Huron, South Dakota. Although neither house was built, Olgivanna Wright, John Howe, and Taliesin archivist Bruce Pfeiffer all referred to the Hoult House as the first Usonian house and, to start the Jacobs House, Wright instructed his apprentice Benjamin Dombar to drop the Hoult plan onto the Jacobses' site. Architecture, after all, is a practice: you get better by doing it. Wright did get better in successive versions, but architecture students can take heart that Wright did not get it right the first time (the spaces of the Hoult House are flat and lack the syncopations of the Jacobs House) or the second (the masonry pieces are not dispersed in the grid of the Lusk House so much as cast adrift). The entry, in particular, was hopelessly divided at the Lusk House after having reached a balance at the Hoult House, a balance that Wright revived with only minor modifications at the Jacobs House.

Wright resolved the entry by providing two doors and establishing different qualities for each. The public way is framed by the carport's masonry-bearing wall to one side and a lone supporting column to the other, then deflects in darkness from the masonry core to a doorway that beckons with the promise of light. The family entry, although facing the street, is blocked by the automobile and is pushed far to the left, deep within the carport. Entering here, we are redirected from the bedrooms by the offset wall of the master bedroom and drawn to the right by light streaming from the windows encircling the dining nook and, still further, the floor-to-ceiling glazing of the living area. With great finesse and in little space, Wright granted this little house both a dramatic entry for dignitaries and a separate path for the barefoot wanderings of its family. The separate paths are set up by the

2.6

Street façade

placement of the automobile, which is integrated with family life rather than penned in a separate oversized barn. It seems appropriate that Wright deployed this new machine, the automobile, to negotiate the older machinery of the house: bathroom, kitchen, furnace, and fireplace.

Yet things are never just one thing at the Jacobs House. An understanding of the brick core as a mechanical shaft is too simple. Much like his rival Le Corbusier, Wright believed that a building should facilitate human activities, not impede them; act, to use Corbusier's oft-repeated phrase, like a "machine for living." Unlike doctrinaire modernists, however, Wright (and Le Corbusier, for that matter) did not believe that this is all a building should do. Wright insisted that his operative metaphor was the tree, not the machine, and the little brick core of the Jacobs House is eager to leap beyond its functional assignment. The core, after all, is yoked to the fireplace: the centering icon of a Wright house, its flame warming the family and offering a primitive setting for the family's timeless dramas. Entering the kitchen and bathroom, however, we are surprised by their towering height; their ceilings are set at 11 feet 7 inches and are accented by clerestory lighting. Throughout his career, Wright defined domestic space as horizontal extensions drawn outward with perimeter windows and consecrated communal space as introverted vertical extrusions capped with skylights. We are startled by the sonorous tones visited upon these banal activities: cookstoves and toilets as vehicles for transcendence? Surely, Wright teases us with irony. I think not.

The kitchen is easiest to come to terms with: Wright pushed it from the back of the Victorian house where it hid servants, odors, and refuse. Now, with a liberated family dynamic (and a depressed family economic), Wright pulled the kitchen into the home's revolving center where it became a domestic pilothouse from which to monitor the family's comings and goings, direct food to and from the dining table, and survey the garden. Although we might protest the stereotypical roles of wife (cooking in the kitchen) and husband (at the fire with pipe and newspaper), there is no doubt that this little kitchen, its new laborsaving appliances gleaming under heraldic light, is a place of power.

But what of the bathroom, so often scrubbed clean with the hygienic fastidiousness of modernism? Granted, Wright concerned himself with its equipment, designing a custom bathtub for the Jacobses. Yet there's more: this is a house for a young family, and the bathroom is not simply a place for disposing waste but is the locus of low comedy: odiferous eminences greeted by incredulous guffaws; sexual posturing checked by the blackmail of childhood bathing movies; and Oedipal dramas leavened by the comic reversals of toilet training as parents crouch in attendance upon enthroned youth. Paradoxically, the bathroom is also the setting for a domestic sublime as an adult or child, in a solitary bath, basks in muted light at the bottom of a deep, warm well. Wright did not simply solve mechanical problems by gathering equipment into an efficient shaft. Wright celebrated the body. He enshrined it in a stout earthen monument, warmed it with fire, cleansed it with water, and illuminated it with warm rays.

———

Although I have referred to the Jacobs House plan with the quasi-scientific nomenclature, *L*, Wright preferred the imagery of nature and referred to the plan as a "polliwog." Leaving aside the facts that this polliwog has somehow swallowed a large stone (the brick core) and sports a rakish collar (the carport), the voluminous living room does resemble a head, and the string of bedrooms and study does resemble a tail. Moreover, this polliwog's tail moves.

In the Hoult and Lusk projects, the bedrooms occupy a similar position in the plan. Yet the spaces are arranged along flaccid lines; the bedrooms are little boxes strung along a listless corridor.

2.7

Bedroom

These tails hang limp, dead. The Jacobses' tail whips to life: swelling at the entry, feinting to the living area, constricting about the master bedroom, and finally popping into a little shop off the study, a study that is broken from the adjacent bedrooms by a door to the garden. Circulation is now a little adventure heightened by the manic zigzag of the board and batten envelope and the melodrama of light as we move from darkness at the entry, to dappled clerestory light in the corridor, to a final burst of daylight at the shop doorway.

The bedrooms also spring into action, jostling back and forth, their doorways rarely seen straight on, but discovered on the oblique. We move into these little sleeping cabins diagonally, entering at the corner to find beds nested in opposing corners. Boards and battens sweep aside the remaining vernacular encumbrances that Wright promised to eliminate: the interior skin of plaster (check), trim work (check), paint (check), and bric-a-brac (check), as everything—beds, desks, drawers, closets, electrical outlets and switches (check, check, check, check, check)—is knit into continuous horizontal bands. Lying in our beds and tucked under a low roof, we are safely nested in shadow while, at the same time, we are drawn out; expansive views pull us into the garden as the extended eaves and carpet blur a division already obscured by glazed doors. A curious tension tears at these nests—one that will recur.

After the contractions and release of the tail, the polliwog's head feels capacious; the living room's 9 foot 4 inch ceilings are a welcome relief from the 7 foot 3 inch compression of the bedroom wing. It is typical of Wright, however, to offer spatial generosity only after a miserly struggle. The midwestern landscape is sliced by the low carport roof above, bisected by the roof's brick bearing wall to the right, and blocked by the brick core wall straight ahead—all of which combine to suck us into a deeply set doorway so that we are squirted through the foyer's dark canal and beyond the fireplace to stand squinting in the light of the living area. This

2.8

Living room from dining nook

happens in twenty feet; the sequence is so abrupt and operatic that we are not so much drawn into the new space as reborn to it. A bit over the top, to be sure (and a ploy that Wright never tired of), but the living space is subtler.

Having survived the entrance, our eyes adjust to the warm reflected light of amber pine and red concrete, a light that complements the cooler greens and blues outside. Clerestory windows relieve the insistent board and batten west wall to our right, a wall that is reinforced by bookshelves extending effortlessly from the battens behind. This suspended library piece terminates at its far end with a hovering desk that both locks into the corner, providing a transition from wood wall to a southern brick pier, and declares its independence, its horizontal surface floating free of the batten's steady measure. Bricks stabilize the head; their mass prevents the energetic movement of the unballasted wooden tail. Yet the bricks also stagger back and bend to provide a reading nook behind the desk, are punctuated by glazing that recapitulates the battens, and turn yet again into the landscape beyond with a final bow to the east wall's glazed doors. The solitary activities of family members enter the loose play of wood, brick, and glass within the measured field of battens and scored red floor.

Turning now to the north, we face the fireplace, and it also seems to shift. The hearth centers the horizontal extensions of Wright's Prairie houses, but it must negotiate a more complex role in a space that resists the Prairie houses' easier lateral symmetries. And this the fireplace does: gravitating to the darkness of the west wall with its massive brick mantel, aligning just enough to its southern brick partners to suggest an allegiance, but not so firmly to insist upon an axis, and offering a low seat for cooling pots, whiskey glasses, or a chilled child so that we pull our chair to its warmth obliquely, not frontally, and keep our backs to daylight. We do not have the entire inglenook, for that would separate us from the living space; we have just enough with chair and fire to

2.9

Living room to fireplace

establish intimacy. The dining nook, in its daylit pocket of wood, is beyond the fireplace to our right. Brick reappears to support the nook and staple the kitchen block to the living area, a staple reinforced by the track lighting that runs above. Each moment is distinct and idiosyncratic, yet also a part of a larger living space. The red carpet of concrete lies unencumbered in the middle and opens as a porch to the east, a setting for gatherings of family and friends: dinners, finger painting, carpentry, cocktail parties, puzzles, bike repairs, hopscotch, . . . anything. The historian Norris Kelly Smith has cogently argued that Wright abandoned all at Oak Park—wife, children, house, and practice—because he could not strike a balance between individual desires and group identity in either family life or architecture; Wright's rants against convention's "box" were personally as well as architecturally motivated. Here, under great constraints, Wright opened the box and revealed a balance.

The balance, however, is momentary. Much as individual family members are both nested in their bedrooms and cast out into the garden, the living space frames the family's solitary and communal activities while tossing them out into this same garden. "L" or "polliwog," call it what you will, the plan cups its completing void, one that we are propelled into, moving from darkness to light, compression to expansion, and horizontal banding to vertical casings. Wright weaves all these oppositions into one continuous fabric, especially the last. The fabric's weft is scored in the concrete, glimpsed at the clerestory, and recovered by the warp of boards and battens that wrap the wall into the ceiling and turn midspan to address the door casings' countering upright weft. Yet the fabric, too, has its bias. Marked at the brick entry canal, we slice across the slab's orthogonal between the coupled brick pylons of the reading nook and dining alcove, and, as wooden walls flicker away to overreaching eaves and concrete, we slip through glazed doors and into a landscape that pulls us still further, tilting downhill to the southwest. We are cast out of doors everywhere in the dynamic wooden volume of the house much as we are ceremoniously directed upward in its compressed masonry core.

Or are we? This final void is not, after all, a neutral formal device but a vegetable garden. The plan might argue for it, but the Jacobs family depended upon this garden during the Depression. And the rows of planting will fall two feet apart—the same module as the house. This inscription will also flicker and fade as the land drops into bushes and trees, yet we are left with the unsettling impression that this pattern was always there, waiting to be exhumed.

Wright certainly believed this was the case. Pattern was everything to Wright: his childhood Froebel training taught him to generate a rhythmic graphic, flip it into three dimensions, and reveal a Platonic order; his Unitarian heritage inculcated him with the belief that such an order united all schools of thought; his readings of American transcendentalists Emerson and Thoreau convinced him that this unity could be apprehended by anyone provided that he were independent-minded and attentive to the revelatory power of nature; his tracings of late-nineteenth-century ornamental strategies revealed to him nature's deepest realities as a super geometry that shared a kinship with arcane Irish and Islamic iconographies; his appreciation of pre-Columbian architecture and his collection of Japanese prints and Amerindian handcrafts offered additional examples he could follow to conventionalize and abstract the natural world into complex two-dimensional images; his enthusiasm for the architectural theories of Viollet-le-Duc linked these strategies to architecture through an organic logic of structure, construction, climate, culture, and economy; and, finally, his interpretation of twentieth-century molecular biology and organic chemistry gave him a scientific grounding for all of the above. Pattern, for Wright, was not a formulaic approach to design or a utilitarian device for space planning. When Wright began to draw a plan of a house, as he invariably did with the simple pattern of a grid, he believed that he was invoking the essence of life—his plan was a divine encoding. And when Wright extended that pattern from plan into a continuous building envelope and then out into the landscape as he did at the Jacobs House, he claimed a unity whereby everyday family life intertwined with the revelatory potential of nature. And Wright, make no mistake, was adamant that "Nature should be spelled with a capital 'N' not because Nature is God but because all that we can learn of God we will learn from the body of God, which we call Nature." This should give us the willies. The fabric is now an epistemological net—one that we are caught in, like polliwogs.

———

Yet the Jacobs House is built of wood, wood that Wright did not want painted or treated. There is, of course, a good deal of sentimentalizing about wood in such a "natural state," but wood in its natural state is not lumber or boards or beams. It is a tree. To get the lumber or boards or beams, we must cut the tree down, strip its limbs, peal its skin, rip it lengthwise, and dice it into usable lengths. We kill for lumber. And then we butcher. A board is wood in its natural state only insofar as we recognize it as being dead. Most of us shy away from this recognition—hence the sentimentalizing. Wright didn't. What Wright objected to was the way wood was further tortured with excessive decorative cuts and then masked by paint. He insisted on straight lengths of wood with its grain figure, or veining, revealed. Wright did not want the veins sealed; he wanted the wood, it is not too much to say, neither dressed nor embalmed. Turning boards and battens to the horizontal, exposing their joints to the weather, lying them down onto a damp concrete slab—Wright begins a process that the lack of finish only accelerates.

Wood, as we have seen, is an adaptable building material. Left exposed to the elements, however, wood will not keep. It will warp and rot through successive drenchings and dryings, discolor and decompose with repeated exposure to the sun, become riddled with bugs, or burn. Thus, numerous strategies exist for cladding a wood light frame and raising it above grade. Wright knew these strategies and knew the risks of ignoring them since he lived in the fetid damp of Wisconsin and the arid desert of Arizona and, with more terrifying intimacy, he had survived two fires at Spring Green. Wright seemed not to care. Given the choice between protecting or exposing wood at the Jacobs House, Wright always chose the latter.

Even fires seemed to have fascinated rather than repelled Wright in his later years. Taliesin fellows warily noted that Wright became something of a pyro-hobbyist, insisting that Taliesin East's fireplaces blaze and leading the annual spring burnings of brush with such abandon that structures often followed fields into the conflagration. At the Jacobs House, Wright eliminated the fluelike chambers from the wood light frame but stripped its protective plaster coating. The wall is little more than kindling, kindling wrapping fire. The hearth's flame, after all, may leap.

It is true that Wright acquiesced to the Jacobses' repeated requests for a coat of linseed oil and it is true that sealants protect later Usonian houses that are, in addition, clad with more resilient cypress. Many of these houses still stand, but their longevity is due to the diligence of owners and preservation groups—not to these adjustments. Left as constructed, the Jacobs House would have lasted only the generation of its family. Fascia boards would sag and rafters would soon follow, exposing walls below that would pitch over softened sills and buckling concrete; in time, only the masonry piers would remain, and then those little monuments would also trip, fall, and fold back into the earth.

Perhaps this is only appropriate: the life of the house mated with the life of the family. The Jacobs House intimates that Wright's vision of the family was more complex than his Usonian rhetoric allowed. Wright was attuned to a house's psychological terrain; he abhorred what he called the "furtive underground" of the basement much as he deplored the attic's zone of clutter and daydream. At the Jacobs House, the slab seals the basement's domain of nightmare, much as the flat roof compresses the attic zone of reverie and directs it to daylight. However, the horizontal expanse that remains is haunted with its own demons. Violence plagued Wright's family: his mistress and children slaughtered with an axe by a deranged servant; his beloved granddaughter butchered with her child in a car wreck; John Lloyd knifed by Wright himself during their salary dispute, the father's lunges exhausted only when the son beat him unconscious on the stone floor. Violence finds every family, however; the inevitable clash of egos seems to require it, and what violence family members do not provide, the world does. The Jacobs House has its moments of light comedy and its interludes of repose, certainly—these are all wonderful. Yet recall how the house casts us out. Verdure beckons, but it is the house that throws us outward, centrifugally, of its own accord. We might now wonder at its warm carpet. Again, recall how the Jacobs House founds itself upon a slab stained red. Wright was very specific about this red; he called it "Cherokee red." It is, make no mistake, the red of war, of fire, and of blood. This sanguineous proscenium is no setting for a bland homily; it calls for Euripides, for Nathaniel Hawthorne, for Eugene O'Neill. Then it calls for its own demise.

And what about the landscape into which we are cast? Here, too, Wright's Usonian blather, his vaunted pastoral, obscures a more profound insight. Even when returning to the fecund embrace of the voluptuous Wisconsin hills, Wright carries something of the "ancient battlefield" of the Arizona desert:

> And this inexorable grasp of vegetation on the earth itself is more terrifying to me here as a principle at work, as it is everywhere, than are all the others put together.
>
> There seems to be no mortal escape, even in death, from this earth-principle—or is it sun-principle—of growth. This creative creature of the sun.
>
> Death being necessary to this creative creature's increase, death was invented.
>
> Is this extraordinary style and character here in the desert . . . the struggle in the sun to survive the sun? Every line and the very substance of the great sweeping masses of rock and mesa speak of terrific violence. All are scarred by conquest, marred by defeat of warring forces.

Demons here, too, then. Demons of violence and destruction that Wright feared, but—rising above his countrymen who do not even now recognize the fear that has lain waste so much of the land that inspires it—Wright faced these demons and, with them, his own mortality. Wood light frame construction, it should now be clear, is the endgame of Wright's architecture. If, as Wright would have it, architecture is organic—a fluid dynamic that enfolds construction, landscape, and inhabitation in an evolving continuity—then its regeneration depends on the fertilizing agent of death. The tree, to use Wright's metaphor, not only stands but also must fall and rot so other trees might stand and fall and rot, ad infinitum.

Yet what are we to make of this architecture of ephemera? It is masterfully done, to be sure: weaving enclosure, mechanical, electrical, and structural systems into a seamless continuity, folding from its interior into the landscape even as it denies its independence as an object from the exterior. The walls flicker like a flame, the roofs go up in smoke, and the brick core looms, only a shadow, as the red slab leaches into the green grass. This disintegration is a world apart from Mies's Barcelona Pavilion, where finely machined steel, glass, and stone—whatever their complex visual effects—set the building apart from an urban backdrop and assure us that the pavilion will not vanish of its own accord. Wright's Jacobs House never makes such a promise: not materially, not visually, not spatially, and not contextually.

What Wright offers is a field of play, a sequence of spiraling movements and diagonal releases that run counter to the grid rather than trapped within it. As controlling as the house is—and Wright demanded control, throwing out most of his clients' possessions and rearranging the rest—the house fades into the landscape, a final and very American insistence on freedom from all systems and the endless potential of a land that seemed, at one time, to forgive all transgressions and to have no boundaries. The problem is that we no longer believe this, at least we shouldn't; it has led to disasters.

Moreover, Wright has been credited with no small part in these disasters; many have pointed to him as the destroyer of the landscape he loved. The Jacobs House, after all, was the module that underlay Broadacre City. Stephen Alexander immediately skewered Broadacre City's "adolescent idealism" with such delicious accuracy in the socialist journal *New Masses* that even Wright was chastened and confessed in the next issue that it was "only a preliminary study of decentralization for a better effort . . . and that, largely for myself." Nevertheless, the studies for decentralization never progressed, the regressive ideologies remained, and the project retreated into Jules Verne confabulations floating in a

2.10

Broadacre City, model

transcendental ether so dense that one wonders if Taliesin's Amerindian affectations included the unsupervised use of peyote. Undaunted, Wright exhibited his phantasmagoria extensively and even offered it to an incredulous English public as the solution to blitzkrieged London. Never one to shy away from a fight—his family motto, "Truth against the World," demanding one—Wright presented himself as the enemy of cities and the champion of exurbia. Critics have obliged him, charging him with the ensuing chaos.

In all fairness—and as Wright knew from his annual migrations between Spring Green and Phoenix—decentralization was not his invention but was an inevitable development propelled by larger economic, social, political, and cultural forces. At least at the start, Wright recognized and attempted to address those forces. As delirious as Broadacre City became in later iterations, it can no more be blamed for the debilitating effects of suburban sprawl than can the Jacobs House be blamed for the numbing repetition of ranch houses. While we are at it, we should acknowledge that a Bloomian anxiety of influence has long worried an American appraisal of Wright's work as successive generations of architects, critics, and historians have contended with a colossal ego that tolerated no dissension and a protean talent that never quit. Well, there is good news: Wright is dead and has been for years.

So Wright burned his fields with a demonic grace—what of it? Wright planted with a deft hand. He weaned his clients of the American lust for possessions, he sheltered them with minimal means, and he turned them to a landscape and charged them with its husbandry. Wright built with great care, yet underlying that care was a mortal awareness of the natural world, one that never granted the architectural conceit of permanence just as it never suffered the human conceit of dominance. Wright required little from his fields, and what he did require he gave back. Wood, after all, is a renewable resource. The field returns.

And now, with the succor of time and at a safe distance, we might look at the model of Broadacre City in light of Wright's original intentions: "not as a finality in any sense but as an interpretation of the changes inevitable to our growth." As at the Jacobs House, we may again see, flickering on the model's surface, a brilliant dance within the timeless field of the grid. Wright did not invent this grid (although, of course, he said he did) any more than Le Corbusier did at Maison Domino, or Le Nôtre at Versailles, or Hippodamos at Priene. Rather, throughout time, the grid has proven to be one the most powerful tools we have for negotiating the world, and, if our use of it at any one time is also conditioned by that time, this does not preclude us from raiding previous iterations as we invariably create our own.

As computers afford ever more complex weavings of form, as engineers struggle with the structural skins and integral mechanical systems that these forms require, as decentralization accelerates with the proliferation of electronic media, as architectural strategies move from tired collages of outmoded building types to more hopeful explorations of interwoven patterns, as these patterns are understood to be integrated with rather than separate from landscape, and as we come to terms with the fact that this landscape is volatile and changing not static and endlessly salubrious and, as such, requires a lighter touch—it would seem that Wright has much to offer us. Wright's architecture is, finally, more generous than we have yet had the courage to acknowledge.

> Goethe observed that death was nature's ruse in order
> that she might have more life. Therein you may see the
> reason why there must be a new, and why the new must
> ever be the death of the old, but this tragedy need occur

only where "forms" are concerned, if you will stick to principle.
—Frank Lloyd Wright

Bibliographic Notes

Having worked as a framing carpenter, I was baffled when I first came across the Jacobs House in an issue of *Fine Homebuilding.* The construction of the Jacobs House contradicted everything I knew about wood light frame construction. My subsequent visits to the Jacobs House only added to my bafflement.

The scholarship on Wright is, of course, vast and varied, but a recurring theme is one that Wright often returned to himself, that of the cave and the tent. The cave, for Wright, was a permanent sheltering agent and the tent was its nomadic complement. Both were wedded to the surrounding landscape: the cave burrowing into it and the tent breathing it. Neil Levine, Grant Hildebrand, and Reyner Banham have all made use of Wright's dyad, yet as a graduate student at Yale, I could not help but be most impressed by Vincent Scully's dynamic orations and the connections he made with pre-Columbian and Amerindian architecture. In any case, from the start, I knew Wright understood architecture to be a balance between permanence and impermanence, and, at the Jacobs House, I sensed that balance tipping to the latter.

Three readings reinforced my understanding. Reyner Banham's "The Wilderness Years of Frank Lloyd Wright" underscored the nomadic implications of sandwich wall, traced its lineage, and drew my attention to Wright's meditations on the southwestern desert. Neil Levine's *The Architecture of Frank Lloyd Wright* set these meditations within the context of Wright's evolving attitude toward landscape and, in particular, the shift from the 1910s, when "nature was interpreted as a constant source of disaster, whether by earthquake, fire, or flood, and it was architecture's role to overcome and subdue these violent forces," to the mid to late 1920s, when Wright's adversarial stance gave way to "resignation and acceptance of nature as an independent force" (xviii). Finally, Terry L. Patterson's *Frank Lloyd Wright and the Meaning of Materials* suggested to me that Wright's treatment of wood construction had a consistency that extended beyond the Jacobs House, one that embraced wood's fragility.

The sources that remain are direct references and I summarize them here, moving from the general to the specific.

My digression on Wright's lifelong preoccupation with pattern is a synopsis of a number of essays. Interested readers should refer to the authors listed in the bibliography as follows: for Wright's gridded landscape, see Terence Riley; for Wright's Froebel training, see Richard C. MacCormac; for Wright's Unitarian heritage and transcendental affiliations, see William Cronon; for Wright's interest in nineteenth-century ornamental strategies, see Kenneth Frampton's *Studies in Tectonic Culture*; for additional Amerindian, European, and Japanese sources, see Anthony Alofsin's *Frank Lloyd Wright*; and, for Wright's interest in Viollet-le-Duc, see Donald Hoffman.

Anthony Alofsin also provided an overview of Wright's Usonian project in "Broadacre City." Of the critiques cited by Alofsin, Meyer Schapiro's was the most devastating; what Stephen Alexander skewered, Schapiro lampooned. Schapiro's critique has been carried forward by Kenneth Frampton in numerous essays such as "Modernization and Mediation" and in his book *Studies in Tectonic Culture*. Although my essay is indebted to Frampton's (and Scully's) description of Wright as a self-described weaver and as a creator of "subtle zones of microspace" (*Studies in Tectonic Culture*, 117), my understanding exceeds the ideological boundaries that Frampton enforced.

For general information on Usonia and Usonian houses, I referred to Alvin Rosenbaum's *Usonia* and John Sergeant's *Frank Lloyd Wright's Usonian Houses*. Robert C. Twombly recounted the transfer of the Hoult House to the Jacobses' site (250), while Barbara D. Kingsbury provided a history of the Hoult House itself. Robert McCarter (*Frank Lloyd Wright*, 249–251) documented Prairie house precedents for the Jacobs House; Kenneth Frampton (*Studies in Tectonic Culture*, 102–105) pointed to the Gerts Cottage as a precursor for the sandwich wall; Donald Leslie Johnson (18–21) suggested apple pickers' camps; and Reyner Banham cut to the chase with Wright's first Taliesin West encampment, Ocotillo. Incidentally, both Levine (205) and Johnson (16) note that Wright referred to Ocotillo as "ephemera." Robert McCarter and, in greater detail, Jonathan Lipman categorized Wright's horizontal and vertical spaces in essays included in *A Primer on Architectural Principles*, categories that I inflect in my analysis of the Jacobs House. For detailed information on the Jacobs House itself, I turned to *Building with Frank Lloyd Wright* by Herbert Jacobs, with Katherine Jacobs; "The Jacobs House I," by Donald G. Kalec; as well as project architect John Eifler's article in *Fine Homebuilding*, "Restoring the Jacobs House," referred to earlier.

John Lloyd Wright's remarks and his near patricide come from his biography, *My Father Who Is on Earth* (99–103, 113). Herbert Jacobs's description of Groves's quandary is from *Building with Frank Lloyd Wright* (31). Both Edgar Tafel (*Apprentice to Genius*, 69–79) and Donald W. Hoppen (80) described Mies's visit to Spring Green. For additional biographical information, I am indebted to biographies of Wright by Robert C. Twombly, Brendan Gill, and Meryle Secrest. When concentrating on Wright's Depression-era achievements and misadventures, I turned to Donald Leslie Johnson.

Wright reviews Le Corbusier in "Towards a New Architecture by Le Corbusier," and Wright and Le Corbusier play the dozens as quoted from Frank Lloyd Wright's *The Natural House* (25) and Donald W. Hoppen's *The Seven Ages of Frank Lloyd Wright* (80). Wright's outline of the Jacobs House program is also from *The Natural House*

(69–73); his nocturnal lamentations and desert meditations are from *An Autobiography* (181, 335); his assertion that "Nature is God" is from Brendan Gill (22); and his Goethe paraphrase is from his "Two Lectures on Architecture" (97).

In closing, I offer a few observations that did not find their way into my essay.

On the dissemination of architectural images: Wright's color palette for the Usonian houses was ideally suited to the emergence of color photography in architecture publications, as ideally suited as the abstractions of European modernism were to black and white photography earlier in the twentieth century.

On the solar orientation of the Jacobs House: Wright often flipped the plan in later Usonian houses, giving the living area the benefit of the winter sun (rather than the bedrooms as at the Jacobs House), or rotated the plan 45 degrees, giving southern exposure to both the living area and bedrooms. Neither strategy was available to Wright at the Jacobs House; circulation prevented him from moving the bedrooms to the more prominent southern leg and the building lot's size and orientation overruled rotating the plan.

On the Usonian house's Amerindian heritage: the influence is more explicit in later Usonian houses, such as the Rosenbaum House and the Loren Pope House, where the abstract figures of clerestory sashes and lighting grills recall those that Plains Indians painted on their tents.

Finally, on fire: Edgar Tafel titled the last chapter of his Taliesin recollections "The Fires," and Meryle Secrest cited Herb Fritz on one such fire:

> *One Saturday evening Eloise (his wife) and I returned*
> *from Madison to find that a large part of Hillside had*
> *burned down—the theater and the wing between it and*
> *the living room. Mr. Wright had lit a brush pile near the*

*building. I thought he might be devastated by the loss, so
I went to see him. . . . He said, "I thought you knew me
better than that. I always wanted to remodel the theatre
and that wing of the building. But thanks for your concern." (412)*

Bibliography

Alexander, Stephen. "Frank Lloyd Wright's Utopia." *New Masses* 16 (18 June 1935): 28.

Alofsin, Anthony. "Broadacre City: The Reception of a Modernist Vision, 1932–1988." *Center: A Journal for Architecture in America* 5 (1989): 5–43.

Alofsin, Anthony. *Frank Lloyd Wright—The Lost Years, 1910–1922: A Study of Influence.* Chicago: University of Chicago Press, 1993.

Banham, Reyner. "The Wilderness Years of Frank Lloyd Wright." *RIBA Journal* 76 (December 1969): 512–519.

Cronon, William. "Inconstant Unity: The Passion of Frank Lloyd Wright." In *Frank Lloyd Wright: Architect,* ed. Terence Riley with Peter Reed, 8–31. New York: MOMA and Harry N. Abrams, 1994.

Eifler, John. "Restoring the Jacobs House." *Fine Homebuilding* (April/May 1993): 78–82.

Ford, Edward R. "Frank Lloyd Wright: The Usonian Period." In *The Details of Modern Architecture, Volume 1,* 321–350. Cambridge, MA: The MIT Press, 1991.

Frampton, Kenneth. "Frank Lloyd Wright and the Text-Tile Tectonic." In *Studies in Tectonic Culture: The Poetics of Construction in Nineteenth and Twentieth Century Architecture,* ed. John Cava, 93–120. Cambridge, MA: The MIT Press, 1995.

Frampton, Kenneth. "Modernization and Mediation: Frank Lloyd Wright and the Impact of Technology." In *Frank Lloyd Wright: Architect,* ed. Terence Riley with Peter Reed, 58–79. New York: MOMA and Harry N. Abrams, 1994.

Gill, Brendan. *Many Masks: A Life of Frank Lloyd Wright.* New York: G. P. Putnam's Sons, 1987.

Hildebrand, Grant. *The Wright Space: Pattern and Meaning in Frank Lloyd Wright's Houses.* Seattle: University of Washington Press, 1991.

Hoffman, Donald. "Frank Lloyd Wright and Viollet-le-Duc." *Journal of Society of Architectural Historians* (October 1969): 173–183.

Hoppen, Donald W. *The Seven Ages of Frank Lloyd Wright.* Santa Barbara, CA: Capra Press, 1992.

Jacobs, Herbert, with Katherine Jacobs. *Building with Frank Lloyd Wright: An Illustrated Memoir.* San Francisco: Chronicle Books, 1978.

Johnson, Donald Leslie. *Frank Lloyd Wright versus America: The 1930s.* Cambridge, MA: The MIT Press, 1990.

Kalec, Donald. "The Jacobs House I." In *Frank Lloyd Wright and Madison: Eight Decades of Artistic and Social Interaction,* ed. Paul E. Sprague, 91–100. Madison, WI: Elvehjem Museum of Art, 1990.

Kingsbury, Pamela D. *Frank Lloyd Wright and Wichita, The First Usonian Design.* Wichita, KS: Wichita-Sedgwick County Historical Museum, 1992.

Levine, Neil. *The Architecture of Frank Lloyd Wright.* Princeton, NJ: Princeton University Press, 1996.

Lipman, Jonathan. "Consecrated Space, The Public Buildings of Frank Lloyd Wright." In *A Primer on Architectural Principles,* ed. Robert McCarter, 193–217. New York: Princeton Architectural Press, 1991.

MacCormac, Richard C. "Form and Philosophy, Froebel's Kindergarten Training and the Early Work of Frank Lloyd Wright." In *A Primer on Architectural Principles,* ed. Robert McCarter, 99–123. New York: Princeton Architectural Press, 1991.

McCarter, Robert. "Abstract Essence." In *A Primer on Architectural Principles,* ed. Robert McCarter, 4–17. New York: Princeton Architectural Press, 1991.

McCarter, Robert. *Frank Lloyd Wright.* London: Phaidon Press, 1997.

McCarter, Robert. "The Integrated Ideal, Ordering Principles in the Architecture of Frank Lloyd Wright." In *A Primer on Architectural Principles,* ed. Robert McCarter, 238–289. New York: Princeton Architectural Press, 1991.

Patterson, Terry L. *Frank Lloyd Wright and the Meaning of Materials.* New York: Van Nostrand Reinhold, 1994.

Riley, Terence. "The Landscapes of Frank Lloyd Wright: A Pattern of Work." In *Frank Lloyd Wright: Architect*, ed. Terence Riley with Peter Reed, 96–108. New York: MOMA and Harry N. Abrams, 1994.

Rosenbaum, Alvin. *Usonia: Frank Lloyd Wright's Design for America.* Washington, DC: Preservation Press, 1993.

Schapiro, Meyer. "Architect's Utopia." *Partisan Review* (March 1938): 42–47.

Scully, Vincent. *American Architecture and Urbanism.* New York: Holt, Rinehart and Winston, 1969.

Scully, Vincent. *Frank Lloyd Wright.* New York: G. Braziller, 1960.

Secrest, Meryle. *Frank Lloyd Wright.* New York: Alfred A. Knopf, 1992.

Sergeant, John. *Frank Lloyd Wright's Usonian Houses, Designs for Moderate Cost One-Family Homes.* Oxford: Phaidon Press, 1976.

Smith, Norris Kelly. *Frank Lloyd Wright; A Study in Architectural Content.* Englewood Cliffs, NJ: Prentice-Hall, 1966.

Tafel, Edgar. *About Wright: An Album of Recollections by Those Who Knew Frank Lloyd Wright.* New York: Wiley, 1993.

Tafel, Edgar. *Apprentice to Genius: Years with Frank Lloyd Wright.* New York: McGraw-Hill, 1979.

Twombly, Robert C. *Frank Lloyd Wright, His Life and His Architecture.* New York: Wiley, 1979.

Wright, John Lloyd. *My Father Who Is on Earth.* New York: G. P. Putnam's Sons, 1946.

Wright, Frank Lloyd. *An Autobiography.* New York and London: Longmans, Green and Company, 1932.

Wright, Frank Lloyd. "Freedom Based on Form." *New Masses* 16 (23 July 1935): 23–24.

Wright, Frank Lloyd. *The Natural House.* New York: Horizon Press, 1954.

Wright, Frank Lloyd. "Towards a New Architecture by Le Corbusier." *World Unity* 2 (September 1928): 393–395.

Wright, Frank Lloyd. "Two Lectures on Architecture." In *Frank Lloyd Wright Collected Writings 1930–1932*, ed. Bruce Brooks Pfeiffer, 82–101. New York: Rizzoli, 1992.

3.1

Farnsworth House from the Fox River

3 FLOODED AT THE FARNSWORTH HOUSE

In 1988, nearly twenty years after his mentor's death, the architect Edward A. Duckett remembered an afternoon outing with Mies van der Rohe:

> *One time we were out at the Farnsworth House, and Mies and several of us decided to walk down to the river's edge. So we were cutting a path through the weeds. I was leading and Mies was right behind me. Right in front of me I saw a young possum. If you take a stick and put it under a young possum's tail, it will curl its tail around the stick and you can hold it upside down. So I reached down, picked up a branch, stuck it under this little possum's tail and it caught onto it and I turned around and showed it to Mies. Now, this animal is thought by many to be one of the world's ugliest, but I remember Mies looked at it and said, "Isn't nature wonderful!" So he studied that possum for some time and commented on how unusual it was. How beautiful its fur was, the texture of it, and so on.*

Having visited the Farnsworth House and puzzled over its strange effects, I read Edward Duckett's reminiscence with a bark of recognition. Mies, I had thought, was the quintessential urban architect: of Berlin and Chicago, Neue Nationalgalerie and Seagram Tower, Knize suits and Havana cigars. Yet here he is, standing in riverbank reeds and staring at a possum. Granted, Mies does not touch the possum. Duckett holds the possum up at the end of a stick and frames it for Mies's contemplation. And notice what attracts Mies's attention: it is the fur not the form, a dense forest of coarse hair bristling with brown and tan tones.

Duckett's story, I realized, evokes the Farnsworth House's drama of immersion. Duckett's stick and frame recall the central architectural activity of drawing: the stick, now a pencil, describes a frame, now a building, which affords a particular view of the world. It is this intertwining of drawing, building, and nature that is so pronounced at the Farnsworth House. Pronounced and made strange. Drawing erases a positivist approach to building technology and, in turn, the natural world deflects, absorbs, and, finally, floods the frame of drawing.

Mies drew, always. As a young man in the provincial city of Aachen at the turn of the century, Mies apprenticed as a draftsman to local plaster shops and became adept at full-scale templates of elaborate interior ornament. Mies was eager for more cosmopolitan opportunities and moved to Berlin in 1905, where his drawing facility gained him entry to the architectural office of Raul Paul, a follower of the English Arts and Crafts Movement, and later the more progressive office of Peter Behrens. In both offices, Mies produced copious sets of construction documents. Internships led to his own prosperous conventional practice, one that Mies outgrew in the 1920s while developing a series of extraordinary projects—villas, apartment blocks, skyscrapers—most of which are known to us only through his stunning renderings. Even in the 1930s, when Mies assumed the directorship of a declining Bauhaus, he developed a design pedagogy that focused on the methodical development of courtyard houses through perspective drawings.

Notwithstanding Mies's prodigious efforts as an autodidact, we could argue that drawing was the only residue of Mies's rapprochement with the world that survived the rising tide of National Socialism in Germany and his flight to the United States. Reticent, yet an astute self-promoter, Mies relinquished the only language he knew. Temperamentally remote, but financially dependent upon his estranged wife Ada Bruhn and professionally dependent upon the designer Lilly Reich, Mies drifted from wife and partner. Avant-garde, but indulged by wealthy patrons and, more grudgingly, municipal organizations, Mies watched both founder and sink. Suspicious of aesthetic doctrine, but a leading cultural figure in the Weimar Republic, Mies found himself scuttled—without any means of publication and with only a few scattered colleagues. Wary of political affiliations, yet reluctant to leave the country that had afforded his rise from stonecutter's son to preeminent architect, Mies clung to Germany until he, too, was culpable. Belatedly, in 1938, Mies landed ashore the very country that would overwhelm his own. Drawing, however, survived intact.

Granted, Mies shared a kinship with American shape-shifters even before arriving in the United States. Mies had recreated his persona twice before: upon leaving Aachen for Berlin, and upon discarding family, conventional practice, and his given name for the Weimar avant-garde. Once in the States, Mies established himself in Chicago, with the campus commission and academic community of the Armour Institute (later the Illinois Institute of Technology, or IIT), and, in New York City, with the support of Philip Johnson and the cultural imprimatur of the Museum of Modern Art.

Thus landed and provisioned, however, Mies confronted two more challenges. In the 1920s, Mies had championed glass and steel technologies in his terse manifestos and had abstracted them in his visionary projects. Glass and steel were the quotidian facts of construction in the United States. Although Mies's American persona became that of a master builder, he had built comparatively little in Europe, and what he had built, conventional construction practices had compromised. Often repeating the word "structure" like a mantra to his young office assistants in Chicago, Mies, these assistants soon realized, knew little about statics or the advanced state of the American steel industry.

Even more daunting, Frank Lloyd Wright loomed large. Wright's Taliesin fiefdom was only a car drive away, and Wright's recent architecture pulled into an uncomfortable proximity. While Mies's canonical projects had absorbed and reconfigured Wright's early Prairie houses, Wright now returned the favor; his Usonian houses drew upon the planar composition of Mies's Barcelona Pavilion. Wright was a generation older than Mies and was uncharacteristically deferential to his younger colleague, a cordiality that Mies returned. Yet their relationship was not without its contentious sparks or its Oedipal undertow. A deft player during his Weimar years, Mies could have held few illusions of competing against America's premier native architect in Wright's own backyard. Now in his fifties, Mies had to learn to speak again, and it was not the English language that concerned him.

Mies was faced with a new mode of building and he faced it with the only means at his disposal—drawing. The extensive commission of the IIT campus provided the opportunity to develop a new tectonic and the relaxed construction schedule of the war years afforded the time. In countless meticulous perspectives, Mies and his assistants calibrated the nuances of the steel frame: construction detail, building envelope, and visual effects. The steel frame became the scaffolding of these perspective drawings, its orthogonal regularity articulating the steady measure of a perspective grid. It was as if Mies entered the full-scale drawings of his Aachen youth, drawings that he described extending "from floor to ceiling . . . you had to stand squarely in front of them and draw not just by turning your hand but by swinging your whole arm." Having entered the drawing, we might ask, How could Mies extend the drawing into the surrounding landscape?

To proceed, we must distinguish between two terms: *horizon line* and *horizon*. Horizon line is a technical term that refers to the line set at eye level in a perspective drawing and to which all the defining lines of the drawing project. The horizon, on the other hand, is an occurrence in the physical world and refers to the apparent intersection of the earth and sky as seen by an observer. While a horizon line in a drawing might correspond to the horizon, such a drawing locks observer and horizon into a stable correspondence. Horizon as an occurrence in the physical world, in contrast, is dynamic and has an ambiguous relationship to the observer. Defining boundaries, the horizon recedes as one advances upon it; observable, the horizon cannot be precisely located; changing with one's position, the horizon remains remote; defining the finitude of terra firma, the horizon extends into an infinite celestial expanse.

Might then a building operate as a perspective drawing does, not only to gauge interior space but also to extend its orthogonal order into the landscape and conscript the landscape's horizon as its own horizon line? Mies exploited just this possibility in his European residences, reducing the landscape to an attentive response to the residences' spatial logic. Watching the IIT buildings under construction, however, Mies could not have escaped another observation: a steel frame can situate itself so that the surrounding landscape resists rather than complies with the frame, rubbing up against it and erasing its horizon line. And with that erasure, a very different experience floods the building.

———

A weekend house is, among other things, an ideal project for exploring the relationship between frame and nature. Like its historic precedent, the villa, the weekend house negotiates its natural surroundings, a relationship reinforced by the simplicity of its program and thematically underscored by the occupant's trip from city to country. Although Mies probably did not need the additional license, and Dr. Edith Farnsworth later regretted offering it, she encouraged Mies to design the house as if he were designing it for himself.

Dr. Farnsworth had purchased a ten-acre lot outside Plano, Illinois, a small farming community sixty miles south of Chicago. The lot was broader east to west than north to south, country roads bounded it along the north (River Road) and west (Millbrook), and the Fox River bounded it to the south. Although farmers had cleared the site in the previous century, handsome sycamores, oaks, and maples still lined the river's edge and a second deciduous growth shielded the site from both roads while giving way to a clearing in the center that in turn opened to fields to the east. Fortunately, the unremitting horizontality of the agrarian plat dropped, steeply at first, to the Fox River.

It was on this northern hillside that Dr. Farnsworth and Mies picnicked during the spring and summer of 1947 and, overlooking the site, discussed the placement of the house. Thus ensconced, they approximated the siting of Mies's earlier European residences. In his first independent commission, the Riehl House of 1906, Mies crowned the site's high ground with a domestic block, developed the near landscape as garden extensions of interior spaces, and extended to the distant horizon with the projecting

3.2

Riehl House

3.3

Tugendhat House

lines of the belvedere's frame. Mies followed a similar strategy in his last European building, the Tugendhat House of 1929–1930. Mies reworked the Riehl House's architectonic garden twice: with the stark steel frame of a terrace pergola and the dreamlike vitrine of a winter garden. Similarly, he doubled the Riehl belvedere at the entry carport and in the living room below, where the space's height caught eye level dead center and cast it to the horizon as floor-to-ceiling plate glass panels slid into floor pockets. In spite of the unassuming vernacular of the Riehl House and the surreal disjunctions of the Tugendhat House, both slip from a foreground of restrained verdure to a background harnessed to a perspectival frame. There is a conspicuous thinness to both near gardens and distant horizons because the residences' formal grasp squeezes both into submission and they lack reinforcing connections—spatial, visual, and haptic—that would join them in a cohesive thickness. A linking middle ground does exist: the extensive park of Potsdam lies below the Riehl House, and the dense cityscape of Brno bustles beneath the Tugendhat House. Yet both drop away, overlooked.

All the more significant, then, that Mies slid the Farnsworth House off the hill and onto the flat land abutting the Fox River. Mies placed the Farnsworth House in the missing middle ground of the Riehl and Tugendhat houses—a ground that offered neither the restorative calm of Potsdam's municipal woods nor the familiar pattern of Brno's urban fabric. The Farnsworth House relinquishes its grasp on the landscape and opens like a hand in a river.

The Farnsworth House's slide is less precipitous if we consider the residential commission that preceded it, a commission that signals a shift in Mies's understanding of landscape much as IIT marks a development in his understanding of the steel frame.

3.4

Site diagrams: Riehl and Tugendhat
Houses, *above,* and Farnsworth
House, *below*

Mies first came to the United States on the invitation of Mrs. Helen Lansdowne Resor, a brilliant advertising copywriter and art collector from New York City. Disappointed with the progress the architect Philip Goodwin was making on her family's vacation home and enthralled by the Tugendhat House, Helen Resor approached Mies through Alfred Barr at the Museum of Modern Art and eventually brought Mies to visit America in August 1937. Within a day of landing in New York City, Mies boarded a train to visit his new site: spanning a stream, on a ranch outside Jackson Hole, Wyoming.

We do not know what Mies made of this abrupt transition: to suddenly find himself in a landscape that, if no longer wild, still possessed an untrammeled splendor. Apparently, Mies spent his days at the site quietly studying the effects of daylight and the views of distant mountains. His comments were restricted to clipped remonstrations against assimilating his work to that of another architect, particularly one that had perched his building high above a river on spindly stone piers. However, in the voluminous portfolio that documents the project, two renderings stand out. Both frame a distant view, and in both Mies does something he has never done before in a residential commission: he records the view in photograph and then pastes it onto a starkly rendered architectural frame. Although Mies often montaged site photographs to renderings of his urban projects, he routinely assumed the view from his residential commissions, abbreviating them as a single, abstract horizon line. Furthermore, both photograph and composition change from the first to the second rendering.

Mies adapted to Goodwin's half-finished construction by establishing service blocks of fieldstone on either side of the stream Mill Creek, and then bridging between them at a second level with a main living space wrapped in cypress and relieved by floor-to-ceiling glass facing up and down the stream. In the first rendering of 1937/1938, the interior appears in crisp graphite, the cruciform columns of the Tugendhat House reappearing and diminishing in perspective to align with diminutive steel window stanchions. Fixed to the windows is a site photograph, apparently shot from Goodwin's construction, its distant horizon line falling on the crossings of the column and stanchion perspective lines. Mies is imagining this space much like the main living space of the Tugendhat House: a belvedere that frames a distant horizon.

Differences are more significant, however. Mies is now bridging over a landscape and taking its measure from a lofty prospect. Although describing a one-point perspective, the architectural frame divides the view into five panels: a central panel flanked by pairs of narrow and square panels. Because of this separation, our eyes do not drive to the center, discarding the periphery as an inconsequential haze. A visual thickness accounts for a distant horizon, a middle ground of ranch, meadow, and trees, and a fore-ground of foliage. In each case, Mies revises his European strategies. The horizon line is no longer the line of release where earth meets sky but the line of the valley floor contained by mountains, and relieved only by a bend in the river that carries our eyes, perhaps, beyond the dense cover of evergreens. The middle ground rises from obscurity, linking foreground to background with the mute record of evergreens to the right and, across the stream, the hardscrabble workings of a ranch: rustic main house, half-finished outbuildings, and ad hoc dirt roads among a scattering of deciduous trees.

This is disputed terrain. Civilization's advance is restricted to the tentative settlement of the ranch and is checked by the creek's waters, the forest's encroachments, and the mountains towering beyond. Perspective affords a grasp of a sort, focusing on the distant main house as if to empower its slapdash appearance; however, perspective proves as tenuous as the wooden bridge that totters in the foreground. Turning to the outermost square panels, our eyes cut the horizon's tether and dart through the dense foliage like

3.5

Resor Rendering, 1

3.6

Resor Rendering, 2

barn swallows. We have not quite landed; we hover. Returning to the bridge, we do not alight and instead slip through the bridge railing, which reprises the rendering's formal order, and we fall into the water's depths—immersed.

The second rendering, completed in 1939 with the assistance of George Danforth and William Priestly, heightens the tension between frame and landscape. The Tugendhat interior reappears and brackets the panoramic photograph of a mountain pass. No longer suspended above water, we face a wall of rock. The only human incursion is a pair of passing cowboys dwarfed against massive granite. The photograph is aggressive in its immersion: its point of view drops below the foreground, its horizon line slaps against the mountainside and ricochets to the diagonal, its release restricts to the qualified suggestion of a bend in the pass at the upper left, and its depth is ambiguous. Only the horses establish a footing in the middle panel, while distances flicker and feint in the right panels and foreground, middle ground, and background jostle in the left panel as if they might be experienced simultaneously rather than sequentially in depth.

The panorama reinforces the strange depths of the two elements collaged in front, their colors overwhelming the photograph's subtle grays and obscuring the frame's fragile delineation. A wood veneer sample truncates the bases of column and stanchion to the right and Paul Klee's *Colorful Meal* (1939) masks the column and stanchion to the left. The wood's grain and Klee's figures assert a vertical orientation to unmoor our eyes from a stabilizing horizontality. Our eyes wander in the grain's dense forest and drift in Klee's dream space where the detritus of a European everyday floats in calm distraction: peaked house, wine bottle, flag, umbrella, fork, medieval tower, dessert cup, tipped glass, woman's face . . . It is, finally, difficult to decipher the space of the architectural frame; its single line of column and stanchion suggests an oblique view, while the rectangular shape of its window insists on a simple

3.7

Resor model

frontality. One point perspective allows a temporary purchase on this unfamiliar territory, but it concedes to an obdurate landscape, an ambiguous materiality, and surreal imagery. An elegant frame, a dense site, and a block of machined wood will all reappear at the Farnsworth House, their strange effects thickened and filled. The Klee painting, owned by Helen Resor, will not reappear, although a kind of painting will.

Reveries of the American landscape often betray the closing lines of *The Great Gatsby*: "For a transitory enchanted moment man must have held his breath in the presence of this continent, compelled into an aesthetic contemplation he neither understood nor desired, face to face for the last time in history with something commensurate to his capacity for wonder." Betray, because most imaginings ignore the challenge of the intermediate clause—"compelled into an aesthetic contemplation he neither understood nor desired"—and vision degenerates into a dreary apologia for Manifest Destiny. Sight complies with technology's advance as perspective clamps landscape into a narrow focus, and man's desire for control conceals nature's paradoxical combination of plenitude and finite reserves.

Mies's Resor renderings present a very different landscape; a monolithic territory refuses man's dominion and the unifying thrust of perspective splinters into a dispersal of sight. Having been swept aside by civilization's hot, rabid run, Mies now found himself in a landscape whose cool, colossal indifference overwhelmed him yet again. Mies seemed to welcome it. Mies even seemed willing to accept that his one surviving tool—drawing—would be most effective in demonstrating its ineffectiveness. Tellingly, the final model of the Resor House slips just above the water, as if inviting an incursion.

How else are we to explain it? Mies slides the Farnsworth House off the hill to within one hundred feet of the Fox River. True enough, an ancient black oak at the river's edge shelters the

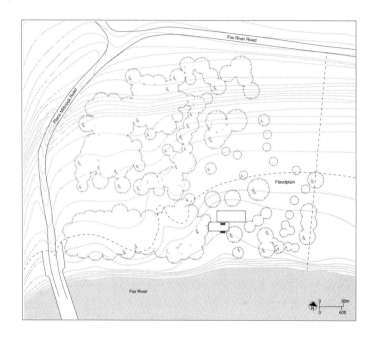

Within the figure:
Fox River Road
Paris Minrock Road
Floodplain
Fox River

0   30m
0   60ft
N

3.8

Farnsworth House site plan
(floodplain shaded)

house from the sun's southern rays. Yet the sun is not the most imposing natural force on this site, the river is. And the final position of the Farnsworth House, as Mies knew, is well within the floodplain of the Fox River. Here, we find ourselves at the mercy of annual floods rather than reassured by the methodical plantings of a gardener, and the riverbank's forested rise blocks our view of the earth meeting the sky and, with it, an easy alliance of perspective and horizon.

The broad northern elevation of the Farnsworth House announces itself amid riverside oak, ash, and maple as we approach from the east, crossing the clearing at the site's center. At present a well-kept lawn, the clearing was originally an unmown field of matted grasses. Even now, the clearing drains poorly and is often boggy underfoot. Two rows of four columns raise the house five feet above the ground; the rows run east to west and are thirty feet apart, while the columns are twenty-two feet on center. Steel C-sections clamp the roof and the floor into taut planes that extend five feet beyond the columns to the east and west. The main living volume glides between these planes, its wood core visible behind floor-to-ceiling glass while minimal steel window stanchions mark the centers of column bays and then drift beyond their logic at the corners. Surely, this exquisitely proportioned white steel frame celebrates the triumph of its manufacture and assembly against its unstable site.

Looking more closely at the house, however, we are hard-pressed to support this assumption. For starters, we see so little of the frame, especially the horizontal frame. Construction documents describe a primary floor and roof structure of steel beams running north-south with a secondary system of concrete planks spanning the steel beams and running east-west. The house is not

3.9

Farnsworth House,
north elevation

so forthcoming: both beams and planks rest within the depth of the perimeter C-sections while plaster ceiling and travertine flooring complete the concealment. The tautness of the ceiling and floor is obsessive. Plaster is troweled smooth, unmarked by expansion or control joints. Travertine, of course, is marked by joints and graining. Yet where the travertine extends to the porch and deck—and would, in any other building, crown to shed water— it lies dead level and drains to triangular basins nested within the depth of the C-section.

Furthermore, what frame we can see, we cannot believe. Even a cursory glance at the columns dispels a claim to structural clarity. Mies did not employ the minimal steel W-sections of the time but insisted on sections with a broader, more pronounced flange. Though full-bodied, the columns discourage our empathetic response. We cannot tell how the columns anchor to the ground, because their concrete pier foundations are buried; nor can we see how the columns support the floor or roof, because they slip by the perimeter C-sections; nor can we understand why the columns terminate, because they seem to do so only with the afterthought of the roof's coping. The C-sections are similarly disposed: window mullions obscure their defining depth, and identical members support the roof and the more heavily loaded floor. This last bit of structural trickery deserves additional explanation. In a final convolution, Mies's assistant Myron Goldsmith supplemented the floor's carrying capacity by enlisting the intermediate steel window mullions as tensile members to connect the floor to the roof. While most glass walls hang outside a building's frame like a curtain and, like a curtain, advertise their nonstructural role, the Farnsworth glass wall tucks into the structure and its intermediate mullions are welded, secure in their structural role. The house, we must conclude, obeys neither the structural logic of varying loads, nor an empathetic association of vertical and horizontal, nor even the modernist decree for separation of wall and support. There is a governing logic to this construction, however; we must look to the connections.

In conventional steel construction, ironworkers connect members by bolting or welding, or some combination of the two. Mies began with bolted connections at the Farnsworth House but discarded them. Welded connections afford more resistance to lateral loads, and welding technology had matured in Chicago during the Second World War. Welding also circumvented Mies's injunction against a nostalgic return to handcraft, a nostalgia invoked by exposed bolted connections that recall the physical act of turning a nut until it is secure. Mies favored welded connections in his IIT projects; the famous corner detail at Alumni Hall features continuous welds over twenty feet long. And here another problem must have become apparent. Welding also requires a high degree of skill and, exposed as it is at IIT, again recalls handcraft, although of an industrial sort. In any case, neither bolts nor welds are in evidence at the Farnsworth House.

With one exception, all the exposed steel connections at the Farnsworth House are plug welds. Plug welding is an elaborate process: steel erectors first drill the columns with holes at the beam connections and fit the columns with erection seats; they then place the perimeter beam on these seats, shim the beam level, and clamp it secure; next, welders plug the vacant column holes, fusing the column to the beam; and finally, finishers remove the erection seats and sand all surfaces smooth. Curiously, these connections require a sequence of operations that demand a high degree of craft, yet each operation disappears with the next. The mechanical craft of the seated connection disappears with the industrial craft of welding, the industrial craft of welding disappears with the handcraft of sanding, and the handcraft of sanding disappears with its own operation. There is no glorification of technology in this curious sequence, just as there is no remnant of craft. To underscore this, the steel fabricators brushed the steel's

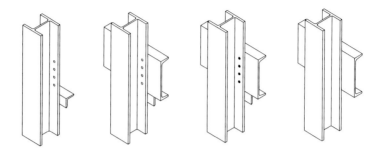

3.10

Plug weld procedure:
connection prepared,
beam placed, plug weld,
connection finished

surface free of burrs and the finishers painted the steel with successive coats of flat white enamel.

The Farnsworth House does not glorify the industrial process of steel production and fabrication; it erases it. What the steel frame *is* need not concern us; the search for essences is quixotic. However, we can report what the steel frame *does*, and what the steel frame does at the Farnsworth House is approach the laconic splendor of a line drawing. Specifically, it is perspective drawing that erases any distraction from the persistent thrust of its projecting lines so that the play of house and landscape can unfold unfettered.

As we retreat from the house and walk from east to west along its northern elevation, a cascade of effects blurs distinctions between building and landscape. Raw silk curtains enwrap sunlight. Annealed glass tosses back tawny tree limbs, green foliage, and blue sky amid glimpses of the wood-clad core. White steel (never truly white) doubles in reflection and registers fleeting lighting conditions, more gradual seasonal variations of foliage, and creeping accretions of ground wash and solar discoloration. And this is only the half of it. The floor's five-foot elevation eclipses the horizon; we are submerged then, the floodplain no longer a remote notation. The underbelly of the house drifts close. Grass and daylight give way to darkness, dank dirt, and faint scat smells. Sympathetic echoes abound: a mechanical trunk shadows the large black oak to the south; steel joists are tattooed with rust; concrete planks secrete moisture; and steel columns step with adjacent maples, trading coarse bark for fluting—a lurking underworld, one of shifting allegiances and strange participations.

Above the deck to the west, allegiances collapse with the thrust of perspective and the parry of landscape. The porch frames the riverside oaks and maples with converging lines of glass wall to the left, columns to the right, and roof plane above. The porch shears the trees of trunks and crowns, leaving them suspended in

3.11

Porch from north

3.12

Platform from east

midair. The trees counter. Especially when covered with leaves and in a light breeze, the trees present our eyes with a flickering field of light and color that waves off the steel frame's request for a vanishing point or even a defining horizon line. Our view dances in shimmering foliage even as the steel frame fades in cantilever.

As we turn the northwest corner, the house announces its methodical progression of enclosure. Drifting along the southern elevation is an intermediate platform rimmed with the same C-section steel beams and nested against another line of columns, which halt just below the top surface of the platform. Simple enough: we will ascend stairs to a floor, ascend another set of stairs to a floor and a roof, turn to the left to open a door, and pass through a glass wall to the house's interior—each stage pulling us deeper into the play of frame and landscape.

Vibrating underfoot in cantilever, the first stair suggests only a tentative sense of arrival, of having boarded a dock. Dead level, the pavers have a long dimension that runs parallel to the rectangular platform; thus, they register perspective with a subtle persistence, one that gives rise to a confluence of perceptions. From the east, the deck shears the trees that press to its far edge, plowing into the hillside. From the west, the travertine's horizontal measure joins the vertical interval of column and stanchion to blend with meadow and horizon, giving the landscape a defining rhythm. Perspective's web lacks the enclosure of a ceiling and a second wall, however; the open southern edge slips as peripheral visual distortions intimate the river's potential for trespass. Travertine reinforces this instability, providing both the reassuring solidity of its mass and the memory of its aquatic genesis in its pronounced grain. Lest we miss this connection, as we turn to the river, we see that the travertine's grain also runs parallel to the river's flow. The platform is both dock and river.

Mounting the second and more solid flight of stairs, we stand in the porch. The porch frames a view with minimal means:

travertine pavers below, plaster ceiling above, steel-framed glass to the right, and a lone column to the left (just enough to check lateral drift). Much as the travertine gathered the earth's varied associations, the plaster condenses those of the sky, mimicking its depth with ambient reflections. Set at nine and a half feet, the ceiling locates eye level close enough to the frame's center to harness its projective force while reinforcing an upright stance. Yet the landscape again parries perspective's thrust, trapping it in the solid crease between the expansive lawn and the forested hillside. It is odd: as we climb to the porch and lose sight of the sky, we do not rise above the thick field of vegetation, but descend deeper into it. Even as we turn to other views, the landscape's strangeness persists—a landscape that we are both removed from, examining from a distance, and thrown into, immersed.

Turning, we enter the house, an interior that marks differences of outside and inside even as it maintains the exterior's material palette. The softer metal of the aluminum door handle conforms to the hand and registers slight temperature differences between outside and inside. Travertine pavers also respond to touch, radiating heat from the hot water pipes buried in the deck below. The ceiling, subtlest of all, takes on a muter ambiance since glass transmits most but not all daylight and the plaster also reflects the warmer tones of the wood core. With this enclosure, the drama of frame and landscape intensifies. Three additional elements support this production: window frame, core, and furniture.

All reports to the contrary, the Farnsworth House does have walls. Steel stops clamp both sides of the glass, their slender sections revealed by a third steel inset that couples them to the ceiling, columns, and floor. These minimal jambs are familiar to us; they are the ubiquitous surrounds of modern paintings. Underscoring their installation are the only visible mechanical fasteners in the house; screws secure the frames. The core, on the other hand, is a trickster that diffuses simple oppositions: allowing spatial

3.13

Platform from west

3.14

Porch

continuity while establishing functional zones, housing mechanical systems while providing for the body's most elemental needs, presenting a clear orthogonal form while sliding eccentrically against the pavers, clad with elegant primavera while linked to the undercarriage by the toilet stack. Most important, the core shoves us to the perimeter of the house and upsets any possibility of a stable, symmetrically framed view, all the while reassuring us at strategic moments with horizontal sight lines. The furniture counters the core's antics and supports the windows' frames. Given our tendency to prowl around the core, the furniture offers repose and establishes a reassuring sense of scale. Mies placed furniture in his plans with deliberation, and the furniture sets up particular views, each relating to a different position of the body: sitting at the dining table, lounging at the fire, standing in the galley kitchen, and lying on the bed.

Now seated at the dining table, we find a reprise of the porch vista. Eye level is just below the house's horizon line, and, again, the joint of lawn and forest traps the frame's thrust. The foreshortening of the pavers' rectangular cut accelerates the view framed by steel bar stock.

Much as the chair stabilizes the body, the bar stock stabilizes the view, especially at the corner, allowing our eyes to focus rather than drift in panorama. The lone column reinforces this strategy, breaking the horizon's extension with its upright stance and dividing the frame into two recognizable geometries, a large square frame to the right and a narrower stacked double square to the left (this last dividing the view into lawn and forest). Thus framed, however, the horizon line no longer extends in width or in depth, and the landscape again drifts free. The column's lack of capital or base and the sympathetic coloration of the floor and ceiling reinforce this drift—the more we concentrate on the landscape, the more floor and ceiling appear interchangeable. The lawn, its fine light texture resembling that of the absent sky, seems to trade

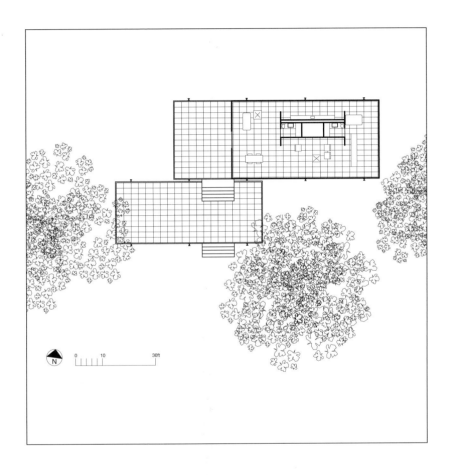

3.15

Plan

3.16

View from dining table
(furniture placement is
incorrect)

places with the darker, heavier forest, suggesting that we may be upside down. With the logics of perspective and gravity both transgressed, the leaves, trunks, and grass are unleashed to ambiguous depths that shift with changes of light, moisture, and wind. The fleeting quality of these perceptions seems to flicker with our eyes' darting search for a stable purchase. And the provision for sitting, for stabilizing the body during this unsettling experience, is crucial.

This becomes clear when we rise, walk to the fireplace, and turn to face the length of the house and the distant porch. A rush of glass reflections, hard steel, and dark water speeds by as our view careens into a slice of trees. Barcelona chairs squat by the fireplace, braced by the core and the wardrobe, which blocks a similar view from the dining table. A prospect, then, calling out the house's most violent view as trees and hillside refuse its most sustained perspectival thrust. Slumping into the broad luxury of the low-slung chair, close to the floor that flips to the vertical embrace of the fireplace, we again feel perspective's pull. The joint of travertine and primavera leads our view along a horizon line that is again scattered by forest. Yet a helpful measure is also apparent. The core's skirt blocks its own directive. Stanchion, paver, and panel measure distance while registering changing atmospheric effects—even the glass's reflections are no longer disconcerting. Entryway and porch disarm the view by framing it twice. The forest now settles, no longer abrupt and threatening, and our eyes, too, adjust. Like a chaperone's ruler, the house holds the forest to a respectful distance, and our eyes move forward, engage, and shuffle into a dance of iridescence.

Eventually, our view drifts to the left, toward the river. Columns and stanchions block oblique views, clipping the horizontal expanse into discrete vertical segments that broaden and decelerate as we turn to look straight at the river. Here the house drops away, and our view relies on the landscape's measure of stacked horizontal

3.17

View from fireplace

3.18

Original galley view

bands: a foreground of grass, a middle ground of river, a background of hill and forest, and a final expanse of sky. No longer a solitary horizontal line, the horizon succumbs to the river whose power is more foreboding. On some days, the foliage's shifting depth infects this stacked landscape—the river seems closer than the grass. On other days, the river does pull closer than the grass and swallows it.

Rising from the chair and circling the core to its northern flank, we enter the galley kitchen and a compressed version of the sitting area's trauma. Yet here the experience does not threaten since steel, travertine, and primavera measure the space, and the kitchen's narrow slot holds us secure. Overgrowth now hems in galley views to the east and west, yet early photographs suggest a different experience; the dense cover of the rising hill did contain the western view, but the eastern view opened to fields and framed a distant horizon of earth and sky. Unlike Mies's European residences, however, the Farnsworth House brought intimations of infinite extension to ground with the everyday workings of a farm and, closer to home, the mundane tasks of preparing food and washing dishes. Turning counterclockwise with our backs to the core, the distant horizon once gave way to the gradual rise of the hill and the encroachment of trees to the north and west, a transition accelerating, decelerating, and accelerating with the measure of steel, the vista moving from release to immersion in one fluid wave.

As we walk the house, gathering views in different combinations and at different speeds, one view is conspicuously absent: the view of the horizon from the northern zone of the house, one that would skip across the water to the wooded bank and the expanse of sky. The core blocks this prospect through much of the house and the ceiling shears it through the remainder. The river dominates, a body of water whose boundary is always in doubt and whose current is never tempted. The house offers an expansive view of the sky only once. If you roll to the river while lying on the bed in the sleeping area, you can see it there. The view is clamped upright between core and wardrobe, as if you might walk across the water, erect and certain. Yet, too, close to sleep . . . a dream.

———

The Farnsworth House does not secure us a distant horizon or a garden's preserve but challenges us with immersion. Here, another landscape is framed, one that includes the salubrious arousal of sensation described by a guest who spent an evening in this same bed and awoke: "The sensation is indescribable—the act of waking and coming into consciousness as the light dawns and gradually grows. It illuminates the grass and trees and the river beyond; it takes over your whole vision. You are in nature and not in it, engulfed by it but separate from it. It is altogether unforgettable."

But for this: midwestern light is not often brilliant, revealing a crisp, colorful surround, but is more often overcast, humid, obdurate, absorbing us in its density. And this, too: if the Farnsworth House divides land and water into separate transverse views—the northern landward views thwarting the frame's search for release, and the southern water views stacking themselves into multiple horizons—then the views along the length of the house lurch even closer. Water and land, like eye and leaf, negotiate an unstable division; they are subject to the Fox River's propensity for turbulent chaos as well as, on occasion, a fluid order. The house stands in the most volatile zone of its site—not removed as an idealized pavilion—immersed like a stone barge. Our senses are charged with a liberating awareness of nature's intoxicating thickness, but we are also cautioned with a disquieting sense of nature's suffocating embrace. The Farnsworth House threatens to drown us in a flood.

3.19

View from bed

3.20

View to river from north

But we do not drown. The Farnsworth House always frames a view, constructs it, just as our view of nature is always framed, constructed. Much of twentieth-century critical thought is an obsessive diagnosis of these frames, and Mies marshaled two of its arch culprits: technology and perspective. Mies built with glass and steel because they were a given, a technological achievement of his time that should not be avoided. But he would not idealize them. Mies deployed perspective, but he seemed as wary of it as he was of technology. Above all, Mies sited the Farnsworth House so that nature disarms both culprits—waters swirl below, forests press above, and strange sympathies flicker throughout—and the house participates with nature as well as offers a view of it. At the midpoint of his torrential century, when so much had already been lost by himself and so many others, Mies intimated that further losses were necessary if we were to save anything. If we could not erase frames, we could erase obvious falsehood, and then we might glimpse something closer to truth. As Mies intoned late in his life, "If you view nature through the glass walls of the Farnsworth House, it gains a more profound significance than if viewed from outside."

One truth has emerged from the Farnsworth House. Mies positioned the house above the highest predicted floods: those anticipated once every hundred years. Yet in 1954 and again in 1996, the river rose six feet above the one-hundred-year mark, breaking glass and destroying woodwork. What neither Mies nor Goldsmith could have anticipated was the increase in water runoff caused by development in the Chicago area. The National Trust for Historic Preservation has recently purchased the Farnsworth House, but must consider moving the house to higher ground. This is untenable—to move the house is to destroy it. Yet the alternative is haunting: a house, which testifies to our ability to look at all of nature with respect, now swallowed by nature run amuck through our willful ignorance.

Bibliographic Notes

Four essays guided me toward a more coherent understanding of the Farnsworth House: Kenneth Frampton's "In Search of the Modern Landscape" underscored Mies's use of the belvedere; Rosalind Krauss's "The Grid, the /Cloud/, and the Detail" suggested a more complex understanding of Miesian space; Robin Evans's "Mies van der Rohe's Paradoxical Symmetries" unveiled Mies's horizontal symmetries; and Beatriz Colomina's "Mies Not" linked those symmetries to drawing and the horizon.

Aron Vinegar, my colleague at the Austin E. Knowlton School of Architecture, graciously included me in his graduate seminar "Horizons," and our many conversations were invaluable to me. The reading list for this seminar included the writings of Denis E. Cosgrove, Kate Flint, David Leatherbarrow, John Sallis, and Cornelius Van Peursen. Leatherbarrow's *Uncommon Ground* was particularly helpful in clarifying landscape relationships of foreground, middle ground, and background.

Robert Pogue Harrison's *Forests* and Leo Marx's "The American Ideology of Space" provided me with a cultural context for the landscape strategies of the Farnsworth House while Barry Bergdoll's "The Nature of Mies's Space" brought Miesian landscape to my attention in a forceful and coherent manner.

My initial forays into Mies's building techniques included William H. Jordy's "The Laconic Splendor of the Metal Frame" and Colin Rowe's "Chicago Frame." When the house demanded a closer examination, I turned to the documentation provided by the texts of Werner Blaser, Edward R. Ford, Dirk Lohan, Franz Schulze, and Maritz Vandenberg. My reconstruction of the plug-welded joints at the Farnsworth House are based on Alan Ogg's description in *Architecture in Steel*, and my conversations with Glenn Johnson, of Dirk Lohan's office. Fritz Neumeyer's book *The Artless Word* and his essay "Mies's First Project" placed technical issues within the context of Mies's evolving attitude toward technology.

For general biographical information and overviews of Mies's career, I referred to Franz Schulze's *Mies van der Rohe, A Critical Biography* as well as Peter Blake's "Mies van der Rohe and the Master of Structure," Phyllis Lambert's "Mies Immersion," and Terence Riley's "Making History." Cammie McAtee's "Alien #5044325" provided me with background information on the Resor commission.

The Duckett quotation is from William S. Shell's "Impressions of Mies" (31–32). Mies's description of his Aachen drawings comes from Franz Schulze's biography (15–16). Mies's siting of the Farnsworth House comes from a Myron Goldsmith interview with Kevin Harrington as quoted in Phyllis Lambert's "Mies Immersion" (509nn20, 33). The guest comment is from Maritz Vandenberg (23). Mies's description of the Farnsworth House took place during Christian Norberg-Schulz's interview, as reproduced in Fritz Neumeyer's *The Artless Word* (339).

Bibliography

Bergdoll, Barry. "The Nature of Mies's Space." In *Mies in Berlin*, ed. Terence Riley and Barry Bergdoll, 66–105. New York: Museum of Modern Art, 2001.

Blake, Peter. "Mies van der Rohe and the Master of Structure." In *The Master Builders*, 2nd ed. New York: W. W. Norton & Company, 1976.

Blaser, Werner. *Mies van der Rohe, Farnsworth House: Weekend House*. Basel: Birkhäuser, 1999.

Colomina, Beatriz. "Mies Not." *Columbia Documents of Architecture and Theory* (December 1996): 75–100.

Cosgrove, Denis E. "Prospect, Perspective and the Evolution of the Landscape Idea." In *Reading Human Geography: The Poetics and Politics of Inquiry*, ed. Trevor Barnes and Derek Gregory, 324–341. New York: Wiley, 1997.

Evans, Robin. "Mies van der Rohe's Paradoxical Symmetries." In *Translations from Drawing to Building and Other Essays*. Cambridge, MA: The MIT Press, 1997.

Fitzgerald, F. Scott. *The Great Gatsby*. New York: Charles Scribner's Sons, 1925.

Flint, Kate. *The Victorians and the Visual Imagination*. Cambridge: Cambridge University Press, 2000.

Ford, Edward R. "Ludwig Mies van der Rohe and the Steel Frame." In *The Details of Modern Architecture, Volume 1*, 261–288. Cambridge, MA: The MIT Press, 1990.

Frampton, Kenneth. "In Search of the Modern Landscape." In *Denatured Visions, Landscape and Culture in the Twentieth Century*, ed. Stuart Wrede and William Howard Adams, 42–61. New York: MOMA and Harry N. Abrams, 1991.

Frampton, Kenneth. "Mies van der Rohe: Avant-Garde and Continuity." In *Studies in Tectonic Culture: The Poetics of Construction in Nineteenth and Twentieth Century Architecture*, ed. John Cava, 159–207. Cambridge, MA: The MIT Press, 1995.

Harrison, Robert Pogue. *Forests, The Shadow of Civilization*. Chicago and London: University of Chicago Press, 1992.

Jordy, William H. "The Laconic Splendor of the Metal Frame: Ludwig Mies van der Rohe's 860 Lake Shore Apartments and His Seagram Building." In *American Buildings and Their Architects*, 221–278. Garden City, NY: Doubleday & Company, 1972.

Krauss, Rosalind. "The Grid, the /Cloud/, and the Detail." In *The Presence of Mies*, ed. Detlef Mertins, 132–147. New York: Princeton Architectural Press, 1994.

Lambert, Phyllis. "Mies Immersion: Introduction." In *Mies in America*, ed. Phyllis Lambert, 192–521. New York: Harry N. Abrams, 2001.

Leatherbarrow, David. *Uncommon Ground: Architecture, Technology, and Topography*. Cambridge, MA: The MIT Press, 2000.

Lohan, Dirk. *Farnsworth House*. Global Architecture Detail Series. Tokyo: Edita, 1976.

Marx, Leo. "The American Ideology of Space." In *Denatured Visions, Landscape and Culture in the Twentieth Century*, ed. Stuart Wrede and William Howard Adams, 62–78. New York: MOMA and Harry N. Abrams, 1991.

McAtee, Cammie. "Alien #5044325: Mies's First Trip to America." In *Mies in America*, ed. Phyllis Lambert, 132–191. New York: Harry N. Abrams, 2001.

Neumeyer, Fritz. *The Artless Word: Mies van der Rohe on the Building Art.* Cambridge, MA: The MIT Press, 1991.

Neumeyer, Fritz. "Mies's First Project: Revisiting the Atmosphere at Klösterli." In *Mies in Berlin*, ed. Terence Riley and Barry Bergdoll, 309–317. New York: Museum of Modern Art, 2001.

Ogg, Alan. *Architecture in Steel, Australian Context.* Red Hill, Australia: Royal Australian Institute of Architects, 1987.

Riley, Terence. "Making History: Mies van der Rohe and the Museum of Modern Art." In *Mies in Berlin*, ed. Terence Riley and Barry Bergdoll, 10–23. New York: Museum of Modern Art, 2001.

Rowe, Colin. "Chicago Frame." In *The Mathematics of the Ideal Villa and Other Essays*, 2nd ed., 89–119. Cambridge, MA: The MIT Press, 1983. First published in *Architectural Review*, 1956.

Sallis, John. *Force of Imagination, The Sense of the Elemental.* Bloomington: Indiana University Press, 2000.

Schulze, Franz. *The Farnsworth House.* Chicago: Lohan Associates, 1997.

Schulze, Franz. *Mies van der Rohe, A Critical Biography.* Chicago: University of Chicago Press, 1985.

Shell, William S. "Impressions of Mies: An Interview on Mies van der Rohe. His Early Chicago Years 1938–1958, with former students Edward A. Duckett and Joseph Y. Fujikawa." University of Tennessee, Knoxville.

Vandenberg, Maritz. *Farnsworth House.* London: Phaidon Press, 2003.

Van Peursen, Cornelius. "The Horizon." In *Husserl Expositions and Appraisals*, ed. Frederick A. Elliston and Peter McCormick, 182–201. Bloomington, IN, and London: University of Notre Dame Press, 1977.

4.1

View of Yale Art Gallery, *left*,
and Yale Center for British Art,
center, from Yale Art and
Architecture Building

4 THE YALE CENTER FOR BRITISH ART, YELLOW LIGHT AND BLUE SHADOW

As an architecture student at Yale University in the early 1980s, I wandered many mornings onto the roof terrace of the Art and Architecture Building, exhausted, and watched the sun rise after a night at my drafting table. If I found any consolation during these interludes, it did not lie with the drawings I left behind, but in the street below. There lurked Louis I. Kahn's recently completed Yale Center for British Art. The building's bone-gray concrete frame wavered in twilight, while its gossamer steel infill clutched at dark pools of glass, cloaked in shadow. As the sun rose, it glanced off the building's roof to reveal a steady march of skylights, a phalanx that was soon lost in a dazzle of reflected light. Unlike any other building on the street, and in contrast to Kahn's earlier blunt Yale Art Gallery that stood resolute in the foreground, the Yale Center for British Art never quite came into focus. It was an apparition, even as the day wore on and light met its clarifying promise else-where. The Center remained in emergence—never leaving the darkness, never arriving in crisp light.

We rarely, if ever, describe a building as emerging; a building is either there as a physical fact or not there. Indeed, before my twilight visitations, historians and critics asserted that the Yale Center for British Art was there in very specific ways. Soon after it opened, William H. Jordy and Vincent Scully fixed the Center within Kahn's twin inheritance: modernism and the Beaux-Arts. As a leading member of the second generation of modernists, Kahn was versed in the orthogonal frame's formal possibilities and had made his own contribution with the Trenton Bathhouse by uncovering the frame's capacity to generate discrete rooms as well as continuous space. Kahn had also performed due diligence with new technologies: he integrated mechanical systems into a matrix of served and service spaces such as at the Yale Art Gallery, and he developed an uncanny facility with reinforced concrete, most notably at the Salk Institute for Biological Studies. Kahn's Beaux-Arts training, on the other hand, instilled him with the conviction that the buildings of history should be embraced rather than shunned for, as Kahn wrote, "they have the common characteristics of greatness upon which the buildings of our future must, in one sense or another, rely." Kahn's mature work returned architecture to tradition's sonorous reverberations and convincing materiality, an assertive gravitas that modernism lacked and the institutional buildings of the post–World War II era seemed to require.

Jordy and Scully were generous, but an undercurrent of disappointment runs through their assessments. This, Kahn's last building in the United States, promised a final resuscitation of modernism with an infusion of Greek monumental clarity and Gothic structural integrity. Both historians gave Kahn solid marks on his assignment: Jordy appreciated the Center's clear structure and flush detailing, and Scully, making many of the same observations, paired the Center with the canonical Greco-Gothic building of the nineteenth century, Henri Labrouste's Bibliothèque Ste.-Geneviève. However, both historians found something lacking in Kahn's submission; although it presented a clear structure to the eye, the Center lacked weight. Jordy lamented the lack of sculptural massing that energized Kahn's earlier work and articulated the institutional functions housed within. Scully was more emphatic. He found the Center "static, trabeated, laconic" and implied that Kahn's work no longer elicited our empathetic response—we could not enlist the building as a model in our existential struggles as it stood, forthright and indomitable, against an intransigent world. The Yale Center for British Art seemed not to stand at all. It was a "lidded casket" (Jordy), Kahn's "incomparable memorial and his classic tomb" (Scully).

I concede that my first impressions of the Yale Center for British Art are sleep-deprived reveries, yet I find them more compelling with time rather than less so. I suggest that we might accept the general terms of the historians' diagnoses without submitting to their prognoses, that the Center's ephemeral qualities might intrigue us rather than disappoint us. In a more optimistic vein (and after much study and more sleep), I propose that Kahn did deploy historic precedent, but not in a straightforward manner, and that he did present a convincing materiality, but not a simple one. Kahn undercut the proclivities of a building he nicknamed "Palazzo Melloni," stripping the urban palace of Renaissance Italy to its constituent formal elements and then reversing them. Tracking these reversals was a strange materiality. Kahn broke with his early fundamentalism: his insistence that materials had timeless qualities and that it was an architect's moral duty to implement them. Kahn's materiality was now emergent rather than declarative: one in which connections were more often concealed than revealed; where the phenomena of sight and touch contradicted rather than supported each other; and where natural light no longer clarified through the contrast of chiaroscuro and seemed to merge with the building as if light itself had a physical presence.

My argument is a curious one because it relies on the persistence of reverie as much as demonstrable facts. The specific articulation of materials through construction is important, but so are the less quantifiable affects that these materials give rise to. To initiate my curious argument, I enlist a reverie of Kahn himself. Addressing students at Rice University in 1965, Kahn intimated his understanding of a building's purpose and its mode of expression, both of which he carried forward at the Yale Center for British Art:

> I think that it is a time of our sun on trial, of all our institutions on trial.
>
> I was brought up when the sunlight was yellow, and the shadow was blue. But I see it clearly as being white light, and black shadow. Yet this is nothing alarming, because I believe that there will come a fresh yellow, and a beautiful blue, and that the revolution will bring forth a new sense of wonder.
>
> Only from wonder can come our new institutions . . . they certainly cannot come from analysis.

Kahn, as we know, was an architect of institutions: religious, cultural, and civic. If Kahn recognized that this was a time of "all our institutions on trial," he could not have asked for a more challenging project than the Yale Center for British Art. When Kahn received the commission in autumn 1969, the town-gown conflict between Yale University and its host city, New Haven, had long festered with the collapse of New Haven's manufacturing base and the increasing isolation of Yale University, the abrasions of urban renewal and the depletions of suburban flight, and the polarizations of class and race. Added to these tensions were the local repercussions of the social upheavals of the 1960s: rioting in the decimated "Hill" neighborhood, strident antiwar demonstrations at Yale, and the Black Panther murder trial of Bobby Seale and Erica Huggins. The larger art world, far from being a sanctuary from these cataclysms, resonated with them. Artists abandoned the conventions of painting and sculpture and turned to a range of practices—video, performance, conceptual, landscape, and urban interventions—all of which questioned the institutional function of museums and galleries in legitimizing art and defining its social role. The generous offer of Yale's distinguished alumnus, Paul Mellon, to donate and house his vast collection of eighteenth- and nineteenth-century English art was, therefore, a mixed blessing. The collection, after all, featured paintings and prints (exhausted modes of artistic production) of British aristocrats (enjoying their ill-begotten privileges) that had been amassed by the scion of a wealthy American family (ditto) and would be housed in a "palazzo" or "lidded casket" (take your pick) and dropped onto Chapel Street, the main east-west thoroughfare that formed the town-university border of this divided city.

If Kahn had any reservations about the Mellon commission, he never voiced them. As always, Kahn struggled to divine what he called a building's "order," an archetypal form that embraced a building's essential human activity. During preliminary design phases, Kahn addressed "Yale," the circulation routes and spatial requirements of an academic research facility; "Center," the contextual obligations of a public museum on a dense urban lot; and "British," the exhibition requirements for small, wall-hung paintings and prints. "Art," however, was the central human act. "Science, all knowledge, only serves art," Kahn never tired of repeating, "because we live with only one purpose, and that is to express."

The liberating potential of art was, after all, Kahn's lived truth. Kahn's career gained momentum only late in his life, but it is remarkable that it began at all. A poor, shy, Jewish immigrant, his face scarred in childhood, Kahn aspired to a profession of privilege in Philadelphia, a city that had as close to a blue blood oligarchy as could be found in the States at the time. Kahn had a prodigious drawing talent and a keen intelligence, however, and his adopted city, whatever its power structure, was the nexus of vibrant institutions that provided a range of cultural amenities and an exceptional public education. To the end, Kahn remembered Philadelphia as "a place where a small boy, as he walks through it, may see something that will tell him what he wants to do his whole life." If Kahn understood that America's institutions were on trial in the 1960s and the cities that depended upon them were in decline, Kahn also asserted, "Availability is the hallmark of America. And it's been bandied around, it's been kept from certain people, but I think it's just there." For Kahn, the greatest resource a city could make available to its citizenry was art, and the Yale Center for British Art offered Kahn a part to play in that availability.

Nevertheless, Kahn began his design with the order of a palazzo. A palazzo is a common museum type, but it has also been emblematic of familial power and prestige since the fifteenth century. Granted, the Center respects the public street. As we stand at the corner of York and Chapel Streets, we can see the Center's concrete columns adjust to the street's scale and taper as they ascend. The horizontal lines of the Center's concrete beams also tie it to those of adjacent buildings, the beams' thickness following the columns' lead by modulating to the urban conventions of base, upper stories, and entablature. And note the welcome addition of shops at the street level, a request from the university that Kahn welcomed;

1 Yale Art and Architecture Building
2 Yale Art Gallery
3 Yale Center for British Art
4 Yale Repertory Theatre
5 New Haven Green

4.2

Site plan with Yale University
buildings rendered in black

4.3

View from corner of Chapel and
York Streets

he also pulled back their façades to allow shoppers a measure of protection from rain and snow. Renaissance palazzos often accommodated shops at street level, however, and architects often study their sophisticated contextual strategies. It is, in fact, just such a close analysis that reveals the curious disjunctions of Kahn's façade.

We need not even look very closely. A Renaissance façade has a rusticated base, as if quarrying the earth below; intermediate stories, which are bound by a taut interwoven surface; and an attic, which shows the most compression in its vertical dimension and is capped by an elaborate cornice that casts deep shadows to crown the building against the sky. The Center has a base, but it is columnar and the columns are stout as if driven into a ground that is not quite solid. Its middle stories' continuous weave is broken just to the right of the building's centerline. Its attic story, most curious of all, is the tallest story rather than the most compressed, and its capping entablature has a reversed profile, receding rather than projecting, and casts no defining shadow. While a Renaissance façade relates to its surroundings by marshaling a hierarchical order against gravity's pull, the Center slides into the ground rather than stands atop it, melts into the sky rather than establishes a profile against it, and is awkward in its proportions, as if it might overturn.

Another building type suggests itself in substitution for the palazzo, one less honorific and more contemporary. The Center's structural frame is explicit; its infill cladding defers to rather than masks it behind a conventional curtain wall. Construction so boldly stated rarely appears in the center of town but more often on the outskirts, not in public buildings but in factories. Yet the same disjunctions creep into this modern type as well. An odd foundation, a broken orthogonal order, and awkward proportions all undercut the relentlessness of the functional grid and lend it a more varied texture. High and low then, the Center is a strange hybrid that dislodges hierarchies and modulates regularity.

Still standing at the street corner, we might look more closely through the lens of modernity, focusing on the advances made in building technology. The Yale Center for British Art is, again, reassuring at first glance: it is a steel and concrete building. Yet I wager that if we asked ten architects to design a steel and concrete building, at least nine would return with a building framed with steel and clad with concrete. A steel frame is quick to assemble and is often cheaper than a concrete frame, while concrete provides fire resistance and assumes an array of curtain wall configurations. The reverse is the case at the Yale Center for British Art: it has a concrete frame clad with steel. Pressing, we might ask these same ten architects which one of the following modern materials offers the most illusive effects: steel, concrete, or glass. I would be willing to go double or nothing that at least nine would answer "glass," given its chimerical capacity to be solid, transparent, and reflective. Again, the Yale Center for British Art would prove them wrong: it is most conventional in its use of glass.

Granted, the Center's glazing plays a shifting role. Sometimes the glazing is opaque, sucking us into black holes of infinite depth; sometimes it is transparent, teasing us with glimpses of the galleries inside; and sometimes it is reflective, throwing us cinematic fragments of surroundings that seem coherent from a distance— all these impressions register fleeting atmospheric conditions and our changing point of view. Wonderful as these moments are, and new as they are to Kahn's work (he was apt to conceal glazing in deep shadow before this time), these effects are, by the early 1970s, the rule in modern architecture, not the exception. What is exceptional at the Yale Center for British Art is how mutable steel and concrete are as well.

The steel cladding of the Yale Center for British Art is stainless steel. The steel manufacturer introduced additional elements—

chromium being the most important—to the alloying process of iron and carbon so that a protective film of chromium oxide forms on the alloy's surface and prevents the oxidization (rusting) of iron. This film is, in most cases, self-repairing because scratches expose the chromium to oxygen, thereby initiating another protective film. Stainless steel is not truly stainless, however; it depends on decay for its durability. Stainless steel can be finished to a range of surfaces: from the crudest, which still bristles with a thick hair of rolling scale, to the most polished, which has the reflective silver surface that we associate with stainless steel. The stainless steel of the Yale Center for British Art has a medium grade or matte finish. At Kahn's direction, the manufacturer ground the alloy to remove the rolling scale, but did not erase the tracks of the grinding rollers with a high polish.

In his brief to Yale's President Kingman Brewster, the Center's first director, Jules David Prown, wrote, "The character of the collections of British art suggests the inappropriateness of brutal, rough-textured sheathings; of fanciful gossamer screens; or of cold, sheer, impersonal glass and steel surfaces." Understandably, the Center's building committee was concerned when Kahn proposed just such a sheathing material. Pressed to describe what his steel might be like, Kahn did not flinch: "On a gray day it will look like a moth; on a sunny day like a butterfly." It is a testimony to the forbearance of the committee and Kahn's impish charisma that the committee did not fire him on the spot.

Kahn may have been less than forthright in arriving at steel, but once there he did not lie. The steel surface's complex combination of dark opacity and light reflectivity, of rough grain and chrome sheen, does produce lepidopterous effects. The steel is mothlike on an overcast day; it soaks up the dark warm hues of its masonry neighbors within the depth of its rolled surface even as it beckons with flashes of silver. Moreover, on a clear day, the steel is like a butterfly; it vibrates with the blue sky and wisps of clouds. Kahn was proud of his offices' ability to keep the steel surface flush with the glass so that mullion, glazing, and cladding are in one continuous plane. In a standard curtain wall, these building elements separate into different planes, and their material effects have a tendency to juxtapose one another so that, for example, our eyes move from opaque steel mullion to patterned cladding to transparent or reflective glass. By keeping the elements coplanar, Kahn's office elided material effects. Glass's chimerical dance trespasses onto steel.

The closer we stand to the steel, the more intriguing it becomes. The distant impression of shifting atmospheric effects resolves itself into the lines of the steel's ground surface, or what Kahn called the "sgraffito." Moving closer still, we arrive at another sensation of depth as the lines dissolve and we succumb to a kind of microfield with its own gravitational pull. We can touch the steel, feel its hard-raked surface even as our view descends beneath it. At such moments, the steel is cool and resistant to touch and soft and beckoning to sight. Perceptions conflict rather than reinforce one another, as if intimating the steel's suspended decay. The steel seems both there and not there.

And here, Kahn broke with an elemental understanding of building materials, what I have called his fundamentalism. Kahn's early and most often quoted aphorism is "You say to brick, 'What do you want, brick?' And brick says to you, 'I like an arch.'" This conversation was, of course, a rhetorical device, one that Kahn often used when teaching. Kahn knew that bricks were reticent slackers and warned his students against holding such conversations in public. Yet Kahn's rhetoric remained within the logic of construction: bricks had lent themselves to the making of arches since Roman times and, Kahn implied, it was in their nature to continue to do so. The Yale Center for British Art confronts us with a very different attitude toward materials. Kahn deployed steel, the quintessential structural material, as cladding. This cladding, furthermore, elicits sensations of sight and touch that contradict each other rather than support each other in a single, coherent perception. Even as a rhetorical device, Kahn's imagining brick as an arch is a world apart from imagining steel as a butterfly.

Let us assume, for the moment, that the comparison of brick and steel is specious. As Kahn remarked, brick is an ancient building material with known properties, while steel is a product of modern technology whose qualities are still evolving. Turning to the brick façade of the Yale Art Gallery just behind us, we could argue that its more solid and static presence is due to the intrinsic nature of the material—what a brick wants—rather than to a shift in Kahn's sensibility. At the risk of appropriating Kahn's rhetoric, I would counter that the brick is telling us that its identity is not static but fluid. Brick at the Yale Art Gallery is not a thick, structural arch, but a thin, nonstructural curtain wall. Kahn, to his credit, insisted that we understand the brick as such: stripping it of a heavy base course, projecting the lintels that tie the brick back to the structure at each floor, and cutting away the brick wall at the entrance so that we confront its thinness and the concrete frame that supports it. Granted, Kahn's use of brick in subsequent projects was not consistent. Kahn asserted brick in all its primitive bearing force where it was an inescapable fact of available building practices, such as at the Indian Institute of Management at Ahmedabad, as well as where it was not, such as at Exeter Library. Brick tempted Kahn, called to his yearnings for timeless verities, and often he could not resist. At his strongest, however, Kahn resisted fundamentalism's easy allure and offered a more complex understanding of the physical world. Concrete was a sterner partner than brick.

While Kahn maintained the conceit of brick's stable identity, he often referred to concrete in paradoxical terms, as "hollow stones" or "liquid stones." Concrete, too, has been in use since Roman times, but it was not until the turn of the twentieth century

4.4

Yale Art Gallery entrance

that engineers and builders developed techniques to combine concrete with ribbed steel bars, a partnership that matched concrete's compressive strength with steel's tensile strength. Now reinforced, concrete answered with an almost alchemical transformation: the heavy, earthen mass of concrete might become a light, reinforced frame. As Kahn seemed to recognize, however, this was not a simple answer; reinforced concrete left much unspoken and more promised. Unspoken was concrete's structural dynamic. Unlike a wood or steel beam whose size and configuration approximates its stresses and strains, a concrete beam may take a range of shapes if its steel reinforcement is of the proper size and—most important—remains concealed. And, if reinforced concrete might turn earth to frame, it also promised itself as a thick bearing wall (or a thin sunscreen), as supple sensual form (or orthogonal datum), as coarse aggregate (or smooth veneer). Reinforced concrete answered the question, What do you want? with Whatever you wish. More than any building material, concrete answers our desire to shape the dumb stuff of the natural world—mud—to our will. Yet with that answer, concrete poses two questions of its own: How will you articulate construction that you must conceal? How will you engage the natural world that you now control?

If we enter the Yale Art Gallery, we can find Kahn struggling with these two questions early in his career. Kahn encircled the gallery's public stair with a concrete drum that recalled his earlier admonishment: "If we were to train ourselves to draw as we build, from the bottom up, stopping our pencils at the joints of pouring or erecting, ornament would evolve out of our love for the perfection of construction and we would develop new methods of construction." Kahn expressed the rudimentary facts of construction:

4.5

Yale Art Gallery stair drum

4.6

Yale Art Gallery ceiling

he marked successive concrete pours with insets; he left the holes where metal ties once held formwork true; and he shaped the coarse concrete aggregate with rough wooden boards. Steel hides within the ceiling above because we know that, were it not for steel reinforcement, the looming concrete triangle wedged in the clerestory would crash down on our heads. All is drama: a primitive physicality of weight and mass that Kahn shaped into elemental geometries with crude timber and then lifted with steel. Kahn heightened this drama with the foil of natural light, an architectural chiaroscuro that accents each mark in the concrete's heavy impasto and charges the clerestory triangle with thunderous echoes. It is an elemental world, one of man forcing his will upon obdurate materials, where the simple act of climbing a stair becomes a heroic quest.

Moving into the galleries, however, we find reinforced concrete playing a much more ambiguous role. The gallery ceiling takes the form of an elaborate three-dimensional truss as if a steel space frame were translatable into the monumental primitivism of roughly formed concrete. Perhaps, but the concrete only acts as fireproofing for the more essential steel structure concealed within its depths. Even this conceit collapsed during construction because building inspectors required Kahn's office to adapt the frame to a more conventional series of beams. Regardless of the success or failure of the ceiling, it is clear that Kahn was eager to explore reinforced concrete's structural possibilities and perceptual effects. Were we to visit Kahn's ensuing projects, we would find him sifting through numerous strategies, often in partnership with the brilliant, efficient, and increasingly exasperated engineer Auguste Komendant and in conversation with his more sympathetic and imaginative colleague at the University of Pennsylvania, Robert Le Ricolais (with whom he could trade ideas off the clock). In our tour, we would find a more convincing interlacing of Vierendeel trusses at the Richards Medical Research Building, a hovering folded plate at the Rochester Unitarian Church, bearing walls honed to a velveteen sheen at the Salk Institute, and cycloid beams cast with a metallic luster at the Kimbell Museum.

Integral to these strategies is Kahn's deployment of natural light. Again, the Yale Art Gallery is instructive. The incandescent lighting of its exhibition spaces is typical of the mixed results of Kahn's early perfunctory efforts, while its stair drum, as we have seen, deploys daylight as a dramatic foil to its own heroic accomplishment. Kahn moved beyond both function and heroics in his later work; the hallucinogenic effects of the Kimbell vaults, for example, are dependent on an uncanny chemistry of natural light and construction. As his daughter, Alexandra Tyng, has observed, Kahn's late poetic diagrams followed a similar development. Kahn no longer envisioned silence, "the desire to express," in a battle with light, "the giver of all presences." Instead, he imagined them as "two brothers." Silence itself, in one of Kahn's more memorable images, emanates from deep within the natural world, "from the water within the depth of the forest." By the time he began work on the Yale Center for British Art, Kahn had progressed from a dogmatic assertion of concrete's chthonic mass in the sharp relief of daylight to a more complex understanding of concrete leavened by reinforcing steel with natural light as its lambent partner. Kahn no longer answered concrete's paradoxes and the natural world's resistance with an assertion of will. He answered with something closer to humility.

⸺

The Center's concrete is striking in its lightness. Kahn's office provided elaborate specifications: a mix brightened with the addition of volcanic ash, formwork assembled with the precision of cabinetry, pours coordinated with the formwork modules, and placed

4.7

Concrete beam and stainless
steel cladding

4.8

Entrance

concrete agitated to drive its thin slurry to the perimeter, leaving a lustrous finish. The reveals in the concrete frame, always breaking along the length of the beams, add to the perception of lightness since they are coplanar with the earth rather than standing in opposition to it (as would be the case if they broke along the columns' lengths). Drawing closer, we note that the concrete, too, is flush with the steel cladding and shares its paradoxical effects. The concrete's finish is atmospheric: clouds of ashen tones drift across its silky surface. Again, touch does not reassure as vision sinks into depths that touch cannot fathom. What touch does confirm is the rough column corners where the finer concrete slurry is blocked by the coarser aggregate and then chipped during the removal of forms. Sight and touch conjoin, but concrete asserts its physicality just as it seems to be giving way. It is like the stainless steel: there and not there.

"There and not there" also applies to the Center's entrance, as some frustrated visitors have complained. The Center does not announce entry so much as vacate it, as if still awaiting a tenant for the final corner bay. It is odd. What is even odder is that Kahn's earlier studies reverse his favored design process of moving from an archetypal order to a more idiosyncratic variation that addresses the particulars of client, site, and construction. That is, rather than moving from a simple palazzo to a more articulate variation on this type, Kahn edited an elaborate accommodation of the building committee's requests so that the plan approached the anonymous order of a palazzo. Following our earlier observation, we might argue that Kahn dispels the hierarchies of the palazzo by linking it to the anonymous grid of the factory. Kahn, we conclude, gets the best of both types: the palazzo democratized and the factory individualized. Well, palazzo or factory—why does Kahn enter the building on the diagonal instead of following a more direct, frontal route? Let me offer two reasons: the first prosaic and the second more enigmatic.

First, the client asked him to. Jules Prown relayed President Brewster's concerns that the Center be accessible to the university and town, and suggested to Kahn that the entrance might be located on the corner of Chapel and High Streets, facing the uni versity and linking it along the diagonal to the town green located one block to the east. Kahn complied with a vengeance. As he developed the project, Kahn eliminated the axial entries from High and Chapel Streets that he had first proposed and, it would seem, the organization required. Only the diagonal entry remained. A low, dark undercroft punctuated by a lone column greets us; we are lured forward only by the luminous courtyard beyond. A curious confluence, then: even though we are on the most public corner of the site, we must discover the entry for ourselves.

Yet Kahn's buildings are notorious for just this sort of reticence. The Richardson Medical Research Building is also entered on the corner and the Bryn Mawr dormitories are joined into a succession of corner entries, while the Yale Art Gallery must be cleaved for entrance and the Exeter Library's monumental stair is hidden behind a massive brick façade that repeats itself on the other three sides of the building. No doubt these intrigues wear on the impatient user, yet I find that they relieve Kahn's buildings of bombast. Again and again, Kahn does not offer us entry to his buildings so much as challenge us to breach them.

Let me present the tantalizing possibility that, at one time, we might have breached the palazzo twice. Even now, the plan describes two courtyards with a third, disenfranchised partner. The third courtyard, clearly marked as a square, is just outside to the west, sunken between the auditorium and the Yale Repertory Theatre. The court is now a rather forlorn pit cut off from the street and populated only by the occasional patrons of its solitary, struggling bistro. However, in Kahn's perspective of October 15, 1971, the court was lined with shops on three sides, banked with the festival seating of stairs, and open on the fourth side to the auditorium. No

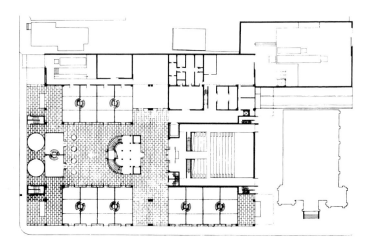

4.9

First floor plan, second
scheme with frontal entries
from High Street, *left*, and
Chapel Street, *below*

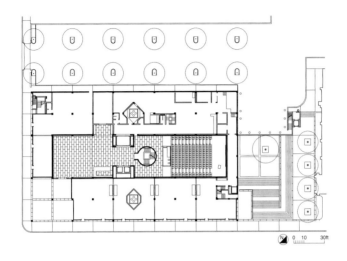

4.10

First floor plan, final scheme
with corner entry at High and
Chapel Streets

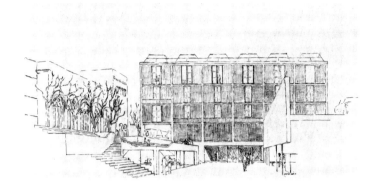

4.11

Kahn's study of third court

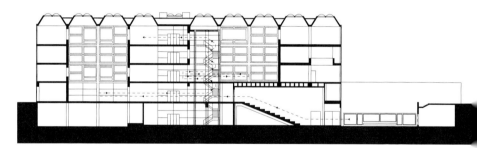

4.12

Section, circulation with
underground entrance

simple court: it linked street and theater with its own amphitheater and swept the public into the auditorium that then became a monumental stair. The vertical sequence could not be clearer, flipping from amphitheater to entry court to library court and pinned by the circulation drum that makes the final linkage to the gallery spaces. And, much like the present entry, we would discover this sequence: a challenge, a breach. To use a favorite political term of the time, this sequence would have been underground.

Having made our entrance, we wonder what we are to make of the entry court. James Stirling once remarked that he rather liked the court because it reminded him of an English gentlemen's club, complete with a lone statue of a knight in armor stationed amid wood paneling. Given Stirling's cockney accent and his propensity for rude boy antics, I hazard that this was a mixed compliment. There is something too quiet and severe about the space. However, we might first account for what Kahn intended.

Again, Kahn's sketches of October 15 describe a very different court. The first level, now sealed with steel panels, Kahn envisioned with open storefronts. The second and third levels, now clad with oak panels, Kahn finished with stainless steel. The top gallery level, now punctuated with windows, Kahn opened with floor-to-ceiling glass relieved by interior shutters. And the roof, now skylit, Kahn left uncovered and open to the weather. In short, a space that is now hermetic and removed from the street, Kahn envisioned as a continuation of the street with commercial activity, exterior material treatment, and the unpredictable New England climate. While the entry court is now a rather pale version of the *piano nobile*'s library court, Kahn conceived it as the library court's compliment: commercial rather than ceremonial, teaming with street life rather than contemplative, and open to the elements rather than cloistered from them. A final, thematic point: the entry court would have had a more varied light accented by dark metal. Even now, the light is unfiltered by the skylights and

4.13

Entrance court

4.14

Kahn's study of entrance court

casts deep shadows. And even now, especially against the concrete beams, those shadows are blue.

A circulation drum reappears, just to the right of the entry court. Kahn, as we know, departed from modernism's open plan by differentiating service support spaces from the more significant spaces that the support spaces served. Odd, therefore, to find the main stair—the most honorific public space in a palazzo and museum—nested between flanking elevators in the building's service zone. Materials further confuse the issue; what this small lobby lacks in scale, it gains in a luxuriating intimacy, an intimacy afforded by the most prosaic materials. Steel elevator doors and surrounds glisten with a velveteen luster. Concrete's atmospheric finish, free of the limitations of column and beam, drifts across extended planes. We press our hands against the rough concrete of the Yale Art Gallery to reassure ourselves that the drum will not crush us. We stroke the soft concrete of the Yale Center for British Art to assure ourselves that it is, in fact, there. Again, touch makes a promise that sight betrays. Sight and touch agree only along the V-shaped extrusions that mark the formwork's beveled edges. The extrusions were chipped during the building's construction and use, and, like the column corners, their torn lines mark fallibility rather than infallibility, temporality rather than permanence, and the inevitability of the building's final breach by time's decay. The concrete offers us this grim lesson with such understatement that we are apt to miss it, attuned as we are to Kahn's earlier, more strident tones.

Climbing the stairs, exiting onto the *piano nobile* and into the library court, we brush outside the drum and measure its girth by gait, touch, and sight. Nevertheless, there is something not quite real about the drum. The concrete's atmospheric surface now circles endlessly. On cold winter days or during autumn storms, the drum even looms with some of the old bluster of the Yale Art Gallery—not by its own volition as it does at the gallery but at nature's behest. More often, and especially in the softer light of spring and summer, the drum seems to hover on the court's rippling oak surface, its size more inflated than massive, its reveals suggesting that it is formed by the chance alignment of matched pneumatic tubs that may drift apart.

The drum solicits a peculiar pair of associations—fortress tower and grain silo. Kahn had a long fascination with medieval fortifications, and, like most modern architects, he appreciated industrial buildings, such as the Buffalo grain silos canonized by Le Corbusier's photographs. Medieval or modern, the drum's progenitors are prosaic not honorific. Undaunted, the drum ascends from the service zone below and sweeps into this, the most ceremonial space in the museum. I am tempted to write that the drum is the most intriguing object in the museum except for its two dark brothers. Looking right and left, we see the steel again, now in the flanking libraries, its surface an untarnished deep blue. Were we to refer to the plan, we would learn that the steel wraps mechanical risers, a series of squares rotating around a quartet of circular ducts: mechanical systems as mandalas. The mechanical towers' horizontal extensions inflate the floor slabs or extend outward as elegant brushed aluminum ducts. Served and service, artwork and mechanical systems—hierarchies trade places with such regularity that their oppositions break down. We might come to the Yale Center for British Art in search of Turner's landscapes, but we cannot leave without an appreciation of ductwork.

The library court, too, has its strange power. Stirling's mixed blessing returns to mind as we surmise the baronial trappings of honeyed light, crafted oak paneling, aristocratic busts, and paintings of faux animal savagery. Soon, however, the elevation's awkward proportions invade the space. Again, horizontals predominate, passing in front of columns that step back as they rise. Again, the columns stretch; again, the entablature dodges its crowning role. Now comprised of concrete beams nearly three

4.15

Library court and stair drum

feet wide at their base and flaring outward as they rise, the entablature is almost comic in its dimension. We cannot imagine the flattened diminutive columns supporting the beams or detect any means of connection since joints slip into dark pockets. And the beams are so light. There is none of the old Kahn thunder now; the skylights' diffusers filter the light of harsh shadows and then the oak adds a golden luster. We are indeed in a court of yellow light.

The oak panels maintain the measure of the column's grid and the concrete's formwork. Yet this is not a stable relationship. Kahn's office detailed the oak to make it appear thick; it pushes in front of the concrete columns that slip back in deference. Which is the structure, and which is the infill? Particularly at the corners, the wood panels rob the columns of their defining role; wood slides by and leaves a ghost of the columns behind. Wood was there first, after all, as it always is with a concrete building. Wood formwork provides the voids that concrete fills. We seem to watch the two swapping places even now, the ruin of one becoming the building of the other. Ruins fascinated Kahn: he dreamed of wrapping them around his buildings, marking history's linear time with a building's decay and nature's cyclical time with the sun's daily rotations and seasonal variations. Here, the concrete frame performs this task with greater subtlety, since a concrete building is always a memory of its wooden progenitor, a memory eulogized by the Center's dark reveals and frayed form lines. Coupled with a materiality that harmonizes with the sun's rays rather than battles them, there is a poignancy that steel joins. The dark steel of the exterior and entry court is the missing wood, wood's ghost, and the luminescent oak panels seem to keen in fading light as they also slip into concrete's frayed voids. This is all delivered with such finesse, a prodigious will to create now tempered with a resignation to nature's serendipitous decay. No longer is it a battle of mass and void, light and shadow, man against nature, but complicity, a buoyant luminosity.

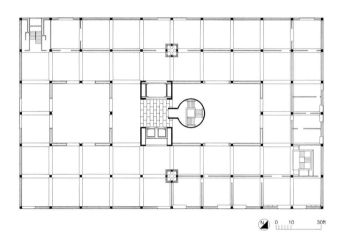

4.16

Attic floor plan

This mood carries us up the stairs. The soft concrete enclosure wraps us like a blanket. The steel handrail conforms to our grasp, ductile and compliant. The light refracts above through the glass block of the drum's ceiling. Unlike its progenitor at the Yale Art Gallery, this drum does not trap us in an angst-ridden struggle but buoys us, as if through luminous water. We stop just below its surface and drift into the galleries.

There odd reversals persist. We are in the palazzo's attic where, instead of dark squat servants' quarters, we discover ourselves bathed in soft light, wandering in galleries that hold the museum's most prized paintings. The column bays establish a modest 20 x 20 foot module that approximates the scale of a grand English country house. We are not closeted in rooms, however; we extend, unfettered by the intermittent movable panels upholstered with unbleached linen. The paintings, measured by the module, receive our individual attention. Even when the galleries open as a long hall, the bays' measure insists on our attention rather than on amassing the paintings like trophies in similarly sized English galleries. Kahn has abandoned a strict separation of service and served spaces, because the Center's administrative offices are adjacent to the galleries rather than sequestered in their own warren. The palazzo plan is empty, mute, without hierarchy, factorylike. Staff and public circulate together in a kind of democracy of use and art viewing loses some of its preciousness, while we never lose the sense of a discrete space with particular effects. It is as if Kahn returns to his first significant project, the unrealized design for the Trenton Jewish Community Center, and is no longer rebuffed by the discrete room or the endless grid; he weds both with a deft sense of scale, light, and material.

The concrete V-beams are now much closer to us. They should overwhelm us, being nearly half the height of the galleries, but they do not. Precast in a factory, the concrete has neither the color

4.17

Attic galleries

variations nor the telegraphing of formwork that mark the site-cast concrete elsewhere. Narrow incisions along their bottom surfaces pocket air diffusers and hint that these beams are truly hollow stones (they cradle air handling systems within their folds). Again, pocketed joints and diminutive columns conspire against our perception of concrete as a heavy solid thing. Concrete is not light's foil but its partner—Kahn's chiaroscuro has matured into a kind of lambency. It is not so much that concrete is dematerialized as light has a material presence. The concrete is out of reach; like light itself, we cannot touch it. The concrete is light.

Looking across the galleries, we see the luminous concrete against its honeyed counterparts in the library court and its darker, shadowed blue brothers in the entry court. Yellow light and blue shadow as we stand in its resolution, a strange concrete luminosity that triggers, perhaps, wonder. This sensation is so ethereal that we hesitate to acknowledge it. In spite of the palazzo's upsets and the factory's modulations, the sense of light's ineffable capacity to intimate inchoate possibilities seems too fragile a strategy. Certainly, the sound and fury of the late 1960s demanded something stronger. Even now, we are apt to mistake the building's generosity for intransigence.

In Kahn's defense, I recall some remarks of Michel Foucault. Foucault unveiled architecture's mechanisms of power and control, but later in his career, he tempered his position in an interview with Paul Rabinow. Asked by Rabinow if a building's plan did not always account for relations of power, Foucault replied, "No. Fortunately for human imagination, things are a little more complicated than that." Architects, too often disparaged as privileged autocrats or lionized as heroic revolutionaries, are released by Foucault to fulfill a more realistic role. As he explained earlier in the same interview, "Architecture can and does produce positive effects when the liberating intentions of the architect coincide with the real practice of people in the exercise of their freedom." Kahn does his part at the Yale Center for British Art: a fresh yellow, a beautiful blue, and a new sense of wonder. The rest is up to us.

Bibliographic Notes

I have described the genesis of this essay in its opening paragraphs. The critiques of Vincent Scully and William H. Jordy appeared in *Architecture Record* (104) and *Architectural Review* (39), respectively. As I sorted out my intuitions about the Center, three writers were particularly helpful to me: Michael Benedikt, Sarah Williams Goldhagen, and Douglas Rae. Benedikt's *Deconstructing the Kimbell* suggests a new understanding of Kahn's late work, one where Kahn is suppler in his deployment of precedent and construction than previously acknowledged. Goldhagen's *Louis Kahn's Situated Modernism* offers another generous reappraisal of Kahn's work: scraping it clear of accumulated mythologies, relieving it from its harshest Marxist critics, and reestablishing its linkage with painting, existentialism, and social activism. Although my understanding of Kahn's use of precedent and construction is more akin to Benedikt's and my appreciation of their perceptual effects is more in keeping with Rosalind Krauss's appreciation of minimalism, my conclusions resonate with Goldhagen's epiphanic phenomenological experience. Finally, Rae charts the rise and fall of the midsized American city, particularly New Haven, in *City*. While reading Rae's account, I was struck by how closely Kahn's career aligned with this trajectory, giving personal impetus to Kahn's lifelong efforts to reconstruct the city, and lending a particular poignancy to Kahn's final efforts in New Haven.

Kahn, of course, died during the construction of the Yale Center for British Art. According to Jules David Prown (43), Kahn oversaw everything but the entrance portico walls, the main stair handrail, the commercial space to the west of the building, and the final configuration of the lighting diffusers. However, much of the credit for the building's success must go to the project architects who completed construction documents and supervision, Anthony Pellecchia and Marshall Meyers. Prown (40) has also described Richard Kelly's role in developing the gallery skylights and, in particular, his efforts to eliminate the blue light from the north's ultraviolet rays while admitting the warmer hues from the east, south, and west.

For general information on Kahn's work, I am indebted to the essays of David B. Brownlee and David G. DeLong in *Louis I. Kahn*. For specific information on the Yale Center for British Art, I turned to Jules David Prown, Duncan Robinson ("Palazzo Melloni" is from Robinson, 14), and Patricia Cummings Loud. For Kahn's writings, lectures, and interviews, I referred to the collections edited by Allesandra Latour and Richard Saul Wurman.

Kahn's assertion of the primacy of art comes from Richard Saul Wurman (1), while his aphorisms regarding history, yellow light and blue shadow, availability, bricks, and drawing and building are collected in Allesandra Latour (19, 155–156, 329, 323, and 57). Kahn's ruminations on silence and light are from Alexandra Tyng's *Beginnings* (135–136), while his reverie on "water within the depth of the forest" is from her essay "Silence and Light" (271). Quotations related to the design and construction of the Center—the committee's concerns and Kahn's response and Kahn's "sgraffito"—are from Jules David Prown (14, 43, and 46). Kahn's eulogy of Philadelphia is from David B. Brownlee (20), and Michel Foucault's interview is included in *Rethinking Architecture* (372, 378).

James Stirling commented on the Center's entry court in autumn 1980 while touring the building with his Yale graduate design studio. I was a struggling member of this studio, thus the twilight visitations. Robert Livesey, who was Stirling's teaching assistant at the time, countered Stirling's observation with his own; the building reminded Livesey of a factory, not an English men's club. As was often my experience with Stirling and Livesey, it was only later that I realized that they were both right even if they contradicted each other.

Bibliography

Benedikt, Michael. *DeConstructing the Kimbell: An Essay on Meaning and Architecture*. New York: Sites Books, 1991.

Brownlee, David B. "Adventures of Unexplored Places, Defining a Philosophy, 1901–51." In *Louis Kahn: In the Realm of Architecture*, ed. David B. Brownlee and David G. DeLong, 20–49. New York: Rizzoli, 1991.

Brownlee, David B. "Light, the Giver of all Presences, Designs to Honor Human Endeavor." In *Louis Kahn: In the Realm of Architecture*, ed. David B. Brownlee and David G. DeLong, 126–143. New York: Rizzoli, 1991.

DeLong, David G. "The Mind Opens to Realizations, Conceiving a New Architecture, 1951–61." In *Louis Kahn: In the Realm of Architecture*, ed. David B. Brownlee and David G. DeLong, 50–77. New York: Rizzoli, 1991.

Ford, Edward R. "Louis Kahn, Sigurd Lewerentz, and the New Brutalism: 1954–1974." In *The Details of Modern Architecture, Volume 2: 1928 to 1988*, 305–347. Cambridge, MA: The MIT Press, 1990.

Frampton, Kenneth. "Louis Kahn: Modernization and the New Monumentality, 1944–1972." In *Studies in Tectonic Culture: The Poetics of Construction in Nineteenth and Twentieth Century Architecture*, ed. John Cava, 209–246. Cambridge, MA: The MIT Press, 1995.

Goldhagen, Sarah Williams. *Louis Kahn's Situated Modernism*. New Haven, CT: Yale University Press, 2001.

Jordy, William H. "Kahn at Yale." *Architectural Review* (July 1977): 37–44.

Kahn, Louis I. "How to Develop New Methods of Construction." *Architectural Forum* (November 1954): 157. In *Louis I. Kahn: Writings, Lectures, Interviews*, ed. Alessandra Latour, 57. New York: Rizzoli, 1991.

Kahn, Louis I. "Monumentality." In *Architecture and City Planning: A Symposium*, 77–88. New York: Philosophical Library, 1944. In *Louis I. Kahn:*

Writings, Lectures, Interviews, ed. Alessandra Latour, 18–27. New York: Rizzoli, 1991.

Kahn, Louis I. "1973: Brooklyn, New York." Lecture given at Pratt Institute, Fall 1973. In *Louis I. Kahn: Writings, Lectures, Interviews*, ed. Alessandra Latour, 320–331. New York: Rizzoli, 1991.

Kahn, Louis I. "Talks with Students." In *Louis I. Kahn: Writings, Lectures, Interviews*, ed. Alessandra Latour, 154–190. New York: Rizzoli, 1991.

Loud, Patricia Cummings. *The Art Museums of Louis I. Kahn*. Durham, NC: Duke University Press, 1989.

Prown, Jules David. *The Architecture of the Yale Center for British Art*. New Haven, CT: Yale University Press, 1977.

Rabinow, Paul. "Space, Knowledge, and Power." Interview with Michel Foucault. In *Rethinking Architecture: A Reader in Cultural Theory*, ed. Neil Leach, 367–379. London: Routledge, 1997.

Rae, Douglas W. *City: Urbanism and Its End*. New Haven, CT: Yale University Press, 2003.

Robinson, Duncan. *The Yale Center for British Art: A Tribute to the Genius of Louis I. Kahn*. New Haven, CT: Yale University Press, 1997.

Scully, Vincent. "Yale Center for British Art." *Architectural Record* (June 1977): 95–104.

Tyng, Alexandra. *Beginnings: Louis I. Kahn's Philosophy of Architecture*. New York: Wiley, 1984.

Tyng, Alexandra. "Silence and Light." In *Louis I. Kahn: l'uomo, il maestro*, ed. Alessandra Latour, 263–276. Rome: Edizioni Kappa, 1986.

Wurman, Richard Saul, ed. *What Will Be Has Always Been: The Words of Louis I. Kahn*. New York: Rizzoli, 1986.

ILLUSTRATION CREDITS